KITCHEN HEAVEN

KITCHEN HEAVEN
GORDON RAMSAY
WITH MARK SARGEANT

MICHAEL JOSEPH an imprint of PENGUIN

MICHAEL JOSEPH

Published by the Penguin Group

Penguin Books Ltd, 80 Strand, London WC2R 0RL, England

Penguin Group (USA) Inc., 375 Hudson Street, New York, New York 10014, USA

Penguin Books Australia Ltd, 250 Camberwell Road,
Camberwell, Victoria 3124, Australia

Penguin Books Canada Ltd, 10 Alcorn Avenue, Toronto, Ontario, Canada M4V 3B2

Penguin Books India (P) Ltd, 11 Community Centre,
Panchsheel Park, New Delhi - 110 017, India

Penguin Books (NZ) Ltd, Cnr Rosedale and Airborne Roads,
Albany, Auckland, New Zealand

Penguin Books (South Africa) (Pty) Ltd, 24 Sturdee Avenue,
Rosebank 2196, South Africa

Penguin Books Ltd, Registered Offices: 80 Strand, London WC2R 0RL, England

www.penguin.com

First published 2004
5

Set in MrsEaves 12/13.5pt and DINMittelschrift 10/13pt
Colour Reproduction by Dot Gradations Ltd, Wickford, Essex
Printed in Great Britain by Butler & Tanner Ltd, Frome, Somerset

A CIP catalogue record for this book is available from the British Library

ISBN 0-718-14731-6

c o n t e n t s

Introduction 6

Salads 13

Things on toast 37

Vegetarian 57

Soups 87

Fish 109

Meat 143

Puddings 181

Vinaigrettes & dressings 213

Sauces, stocks & basics 225

Essential techniques 236

Glossary 244

Acknowledgements 246

Index 249

i n t r o d u c t i o n

Although I've constantly striven for a level of perfection at work, I would never have believed it if I'd been told ten years ago that I was going to win Michelin stars. Opening my first restaurant, Aubergine, was the pinnacle for me. I didn't imagine it could get much better. From all that I've learned over the years — from the day I decided to become a chef to running a number of restaurants — I feel I'm now in a position to give back to the industry, to give an insight into what it takes to make a restaurant a success. That is what I set out to do in the television series *Ramsay's Kitchen Nightmares*. Hundreds of restaurants try their best to make their businesses work. But it's a hard old industry and for nearly every restaurant that opens in this country, another one closes. So I wanted to offer a few of these ailing places my advice and pass on some of my restaurant knowledge.

Whether running a Michelin-starred restaurant or a pub dining room, the one basic element of the business that should remain constant is the standard of the food being served. And that is what this book focuses on: good-quality ingredients and simple, accessible, healthy recipes that anyone at home can have a go at making. I put some of these dishes on the menus of the restaurants I visited for the television series in an attempt to turn their nightmares into a little bit of 'kitchen heaven'.

Restaurant nightmares

Having found places to visit for the television series, it was clear there would be a number of problems to tackle. Some restaurant owners were constantly injecting borrowed money into their business just to keep the doors open, but the more money they put into it, the more they were losing in the long term. Some of the places we filmed were on the verge of collapse, but they all had massive potential to succeed, so I knew it was worthwhile spending time and energy with the kitchen and front-of-house teams to get them back on the path to recovery.

Bonapartes in Silsden, East Yorkshire, was truly a kitchen nightmare if ever I saw one. The twenty-one-year-old head chef had such an inflated view of his fine-dining menu, serving everything in circles, or 'ringed out' as he put it, that I nicknamed him Lord of the Rings. Had it not been for his Yorkshire charm and sheer determination to learn, I'd have been out of the door within seconds.

The Glass House restaurant sits slap bang in the centre of the pretty town of Ambleside in the Lake District. The charming location in a converted fourteenth-century mill spoke clearly of a classy restaurant that should be serving wonderful hearty food. But the menu had such a diverse mix — everything from a classic BLT at £3.50 to Surf and Turf at £28. And the menu was massive — a true indication that they had lost their identity. As a result, the staff didn't know what or who they should be serving: sandwiches or steaks to ramblers or discerning locals?

The Walnut Tree Inn was a different story altogether. The building is a beautiful white-washed converted pub in Llandewi Skirrid, a tiny hamlet outside Abergavenny in South Wales. For thirty-seven years it survived under the owner-ship of Franco and Anne Taruschio, who turned the unassuming inn into a destination in its own right. Warm and welcoming, with a no-booking, cash-only policy, it was a friendly place to dine. It became so famous that some customers were turning up for dinner by helicopter at 5.30 p.m. on a Saturday evening. Those who couldn't fit into the dining room would ask if they could set up a pic-nic on the bonnet of their cars. The Walnut Tree put Wales on the culinary map and was partly responsible for introducing Italian cooking to the country. Franco and Anne proved that if you get the ambience and food right, you can turn your business into a massive success.

When the Taruschios sold up three years ago, the new owner gave the Walnut Tree a new identity, but the formal style of dining and minimalist décor clearly weren't going to work in this tiny Welsh community. And when his star chef left he was forced to run the kitchen himself, leaving a faceless restaurant with no cheery, charming Italian host to woo the customers, who soon started to drift away.

The Ramsay treatment

So how did I go about sorting out these restaurants that were in trouble? First of all I had to identify their mistakes and enhance their strengths. Everyone knows I speak my mind, and there was no way I was going to pussyfoot around the issues. If the chef wasn't up to scratch, I told him so. If the waiter had bad breath, he was the first to know. And if the owner wasn't listening to my advice, well, then it was up to him.

But I've never been the kind of person to say 'I told you so.' I wanted to get my hands dirty, so as well as working with the head chefs, I took orders from customers, scrubbed filthy kitchen walls, emptied bins and chopped vegetables. I went in there in my typical style at 1000 miles an hour, and I don't think they knew what had hit them. At each place I gave them their own individual set of challenges, but the first thing they had to do was cook me their three favourite dishes – a starter, main course and pudding. This immediately revealed a lot about the kitchen – not only the standard of food, but the way it was presented and the descriptions on the menu.

At Bonapartes I was presented with a tuna steak that was garnished with bought-in chilli sauce from the local deli. It was so hot it burned my mouth and ruined my tastebuds for anything else that was to follow. And then, when I invited the chef to take part in a blind tasting, it turned out he couldn't even tell the difference between pork, beef and lamb! I soon established that if the restaurant was going to succeed in this small Yorkshire town, he'd have to give up his fancy French food and concentrate on the basics, such as French onion soup (see page 96), beef and ale pie and crème brûlée (see page 184).

The Glass House duck cakes with chilli jam should really have been renamed camel's bollocks because that's exactly what they looked like! Not only that, but when I bit into one, a 3-inch shard of duck bone lodged firmly between my teeth and could so easily have wedged itself in the back of some unsuspecting customer's throat. I immediately took that off the menu and replaced it with a beautiful Crispy duck salad (see page 28). I also wanted to bring to their attention all the wonderful local produce that was so easily available to them, at affordable prices. I decided to replace their Thai fish cakes with Fish pie (see page 127), using local Windermere char, salmon, haddock and beautiful prawns. We also did a Stuffed loin of roast suckling pig with crispy crackling (see page 146) using local pigs from a supplier down the road. By doing this we were able to reduce the prices and could focus the menu towards people who would appreciate good local food in a beautiful setting. A great Caesar salad (see page 18) and Braised shank of lamb with parsnip purée (see page 148) are the sort of dishes that a restaurant like the Glass House should have been serving.

The Walnut Tree had a completely different dilemma on its hands. There was no head chef running the kitchen at all! The manager was serving and cooking at the same time, and it was an absolute nightmare. He would start by serving up the Brasola, then he would run over to put the finishing touches to the tortellini, then run back to dress the tomato salad. And in between all of this he would be dashing out to the restaurant to take orders. It's the role of the head chef to inject energy and pride into everything he does and encourage his kitchen brigade to support him. But when he's out on the floor taking orders, then his cooks aren't being directed and his kitchen isn't functioning to its full capacity. So I guess it came as no real surprise that the classic Italian fish stew I was served — a dish that had been on the menu since Franco Taruschio's days — was a muddy medley of tough fish. Not only that, it was gritty, because no one had bothered to scrape the barnacles off the mussels and in the cooking process they had turned to grit. There's absolutely no excuse for lazy cooking, but without a head chef in the kitchen to oversee and lead the team, small but important tasks, such as cleaning the mussels, were being overlooked. But if you do fancy fish stew, I've included my own recipe in this book. It's a Classic bouillabaisse (see page 138), a traditional Mediterranean dish that's so easy to make and absolutely sumptuous. And I promise no grit!

The recipes

My main aim for all these venues was to make the food on their menus hearty, rustic and countrified. Recipes like tender Smoked ham hock with celeriac, apple and endive salad (see page 26) or Pumpkin and parmesan soup (see page 98) are perfect. Or delicious open sandwiches like Mackerel with a warm potato salad (see page 50) or Roasted suckling pig with coleslaw and rocket on granary (see page 47) fit the bill as well. Poached sea trout with asparagus and mint hollandaise (see page 115) or Sirloin of beef with roasted Charlotte potatoes and red wine shallots (see page 156) . . . perfect. And I just can't resist puddings like Chocolate mousse (see page 196) or Bread and butter pudding (see page 208).

These are just a few of the recipes you'll find within the pages of this book. And now you can try them all at home!

salads

'The thing to remember with salads is not to fuss over them too much and always to use the best, freshest ingredients you can get hold of'

I've always been a big salad fan — I think they give balance to a meal. I enjoy having a salad to start, as it's a nice lead-in to a simple lunch or even a many-coursed dinner — and it doesn't allow you to become too over-indulged early on. A really good way of introducing kids to the idea is to let them try a warm, simple Caesar salad, or a salad of grilled vegetables, which gives another dimension of flavour. Warm salads, like the smoked ham hock on page 26, are a nice twist and give you something a bit different from the basic green salad.

Caesar salad is a great test for any chef to make properly as it really doesn't need much messing with. When I went along to see how they were doing things at the Glass House restaurant, their Caesar salad was just disastrous. I saw them making it with the most awful leaves, like radicchio, dainty oakleaf, the bitter ends of frisée, the dirty outside leaves from baby gem lettuces, and lollo rosso. As well as using the wrong leaves, the chef ran out of dressed salad and to my horror he opened the fridge door, grabbed a handful of undressed leaves and just wedged a little pile of them underneath the dressed leaves on the plate. He was running behind schedule and didn't realize he was being watched. Then he chucked the hearts of the baby gems in the bin — I couldn't understand this at all, as they are the best part, with all the flavour. Finally he squashed it all down with his hands. Absolutely terrible — I was completely shocked.

FILLET OF TROUT ROASTED WITH LEMON AND CORIANDER, WITH SPICY COUSCOUS

Trout are full of flavour — the brown ones are smaller and more difficult to get hold of, but their flavour has no equal. The secret when using trout is to cook it with its skin side down so that it crisps up. The idea behind the couscous is Moroccan — it is such a good accompaniment. When it's served warm with lemon and coriander seeds and plum tomatoes it's lovely, but it can also be made hours in advance and kept at room temperature.

SERVES 4
olive oil / 4 x 150g trout fillets, skin left on / 12 slices of lemon confit (see page 235) / coriander seeds / 150g couscous / 300ml chicken stock or water / sea salt and freshly ground black pepper / 2 tablespoons fresh coriander, chopped / 2 tablespoons fresh basil, chopped / 3 large plum tomatoes, skinned, deseeded and diced / Tabasco sauce / classic vinaigrette (see page 217)

In a little oil, pan-fry the trout fillets skin side down until crisp, then turn them over on to the flesh side and lay 3 lemon confit slices on the skin of each. Continue to cook for a minute — the oil should be hot enough so that it's just smoking, but not so hot that the fish scorches. Put enough coriander seeds into an empty pepper mill to grind a few times over the fish. Baste the fish with the hot oil to caramelize the lemon, then set aside.

Meanwhile, put the couscous into a bowl and pour on the hot chicken stock or water. Add a teaspoon of salt and a drizzle of olive oil. Soak for approximately 20 minutes, _covered,_ stirring it occasionally with a fork. When the couscous is light and fluffy, add the chopped herbs, diced tomato and a few drops of Tabasco. Season with salt and pepper, then divide between four plates. Place a trout fillet on top of each mound of couscous and drizzle a little vinaigrette over and around.

10 mins is usually enough for couscous. Bulgur wheat takes is nice.

THE ULTIMATE CAESAR SALAD

After seeing the mess they made of Caesar salad at the Glass House, I gave the chef this recipe, which is my interpretation. I've used lovely grilled pancetta, with maple syrup. If you can't get baby gems then use iceberg lettuce. However, there is a lot of flavour in baby gems and the good thing about them is that their leaves are robust so you can dress them without over-bruising. The secret of success is to roll the leaves around the bowl to coat them in the dressing so your hands don't bash them up. The less manhandling you do, the better. The second key element is to make sure your dressing is made with a few drops of hot water because if it becomes too thick it will be too heavy on the palate. You want it to be creamy and the Parmesan will help to thicken it — the best thing is that it doesn't need too much care and attention. This is a lovely salad that can work equally well as a starter or a main course. At the Glass House we served it with warm poached egg — fantastic and so easy to do.

SERVES 4
4 baby gem lettuces / 1 small ciabatta loaf / olive oil / 350g trimmed pancetta, sliced thinly / maple syrup / 4 soft-poached free-range eggs (see page 236) / salt and freshly ground black pepper / 250g fresh anchovy fillets / Parmesan cheese shavings

CAESAR DRESSING
2 small cloves of garlic / 25g finely grated Parmesan cheese / 3 whole eggs / 1 tablespoon Dijon mustard / juice of 1 lemon / 5 fresh anchovy fillets / 565ml olive oil / sea salt

Preheat the oven to 180°C/350°F/gas 4. To make the dressing blend all the ingredients, except the oil and salt, in a liquidizer. When smooth, slowly add the oil, adding a little hot water. Season with a little salt — you won't need much, as the anchovies and Parmesan are salty.

Cut the baby gems lengthways into quarters. Cut 4 thick slices of ciabatta and drizzle with oil. Chargrill or toast these and place them in the bottom of a large serving bowl. Lay the pancetta slices on a piece of greaseproof paper on a baking tray, and cover with another sheet of paper. Place a heavy baking tray on top to weight it down, and bake in the preheated oven until golden and crisp. Remove the top baking tray and the grease-proof paper, and brush the pancetta slices with a little maple syrup.

Toss the baby gems in the dressing and place on and around the ciabatta slices. Season your warm poached eggs and place on top with the pancetta slices and anchovy fillets. Shave some fresh Parmesan over and then add a little more dressing.

POACHED SALMON NIÇOISE WITH
BOILED QUAIL'S EGGS

Salade niçoise has to be the biggest bastardized salad ever. The idea here is to tone it down and simplify it by using salmon instead of fresh tuna, which is not always easy to get hold of. When you see this on menus up and down the country it's usually made with tinned tuna – that's OK for using in sandwiches but not really for this salad. This is a healthy way with salmon, and the potatoes, eggs, beans and tomatoes give it a nice easy-going Mediterranean feel. The salmon can be poached in advance, but don't overcook it.

SERVES 4
8 large new potatoes, boiled and roughly diced / 16 quail's eggs, soft-boiled and shelled or 4 hen's eggs, soft-boiled and quartered / 300g fine French beans, blanched and refreshed / 24 cherry tomatoes, halved / 24 plump black olives / 2 large shallots, sliced into rings / sea salt and freshly ground black pepper / classic vinaigrette (see page 217) / 4 x 150g salmon fillets, skinned and boned / a small handful of fresh basil, leaves picked / thick mayonnaise to serve (see page 228)

POACHING LIQUOR
1.5 litres fish stock (see page 233) or water / 1 sprig of fresh thyme / a few fresh basil stalks / 2–3 slices of lemon / 2 sticks of lemon grass, roughly chopped / a pinch of sea salt

Mix the first six ingredients in a large bowl and season well. Glaze generously with the vinai-grette and divide between four serving bowls. Meanwhile, bring the poaching ingredients to the boil in a large pan and simmer for 15–20 minutes so the flavours infuse. Bring back to the boil and add the seasoned salmon fillets. Poach these gently for 4–5 minutes, then remove the pan from the heat and leave to cool for a couple of minutes. Remove the salmon from the liquid – it should still be slightly pink in the middle – and flake one fillet into each salad bowl. Tear a few fresh basil leaves over and serve with thick mayonnaise.

WARM ORIENTAL MARINATED CHICKEN WITH KING PRAWNS AND POSH PRAWN TOASTS

This is great as a main course salad or a big party salad that everyone can tuck into. If you can't get hold of pak choi, a beautiful Chinese cabbage – big and white – works just as well. The glaze gives a lovely finish – it caramelizes on the chicken and has a lovely sweet sour taste. With the prawns, as with any robust fish like monkfish or scallops, sprinkling with five-spice or curry powder and salt gives a general seasoning and a nice golden colour. This is how we season most of our fish in the restaurants and it's a good idea to do this at home too – it gives the fish a good colour, which you could otherwise only get by roasting it or cooking it for a long time. This way you get the colour and the fish remains nice and moist. The prawns are perfect done like this, and the beauty of it is that they take hardly any time to cook.

SERVES 4

4 x 500–600g poussins / 6–8 tablespoons olive oil / sea salt and freshly ground black pepper / 75g melted butter / 16 raw king prawns, peeled / 1 teaspoon five-spice or curry powder / 8 heads of baby pak choi / 2 tablespoons dark soy sauce / 100ml honey, soy and sesame dressing (see page 219) / 1 egg white / 1 tablespoon double cream / a grating of nutmeg / a few drops of lemon juice / 4 mini baguettes, sliced diagonally / sesame seeds

Preheat the oven to 190°C/375°F/gas 5. Brown the poussins in a pan on the hob with 2 tablespoons of hot oil and season well. Place in a roasting tray, pour over the melted butter, and cook in the preheated oven for 15-20 minutes until golden and cooked through. Meanwhile, take 8 prawns and sprinkle them with a teaspoon of salt and the five-spice or curry powder. Toss together to coat. When the poussins are done, set them aside to rest for 5 minutes and then remove the legs and breasts. Keep the breasts whole but cut the legs into two pieces through the thigh joint. Trim the pak choi and sauté whole in 2 tablespoons of oil. Drizzle generously with soy sauce and some of the soy and sesame dressing.

In a food processor purée the remaining prawns until smooth – it doesn't matter if you are left with a few odd lumps. Add a pinch of salt and the egg white, then blend again. Add the cream, the grated nutmeg and a squeeze of lemon. Give it a quick blitz again and then season. Chill the purée for 10 minutes to let it firm up slightly – it's much easier to spread if you do this. Spread the purée generously on to thick slices of mini baguette and then dip into the sesame seeds. In a non-stick pan, heat 2 more tablespoons of oil and fry the prawn toasts, purée side down first. When the sesame seeds are toasted and golden brown, flip the toasts over and fry the other side for a couple of minutes.

Sauté the whole prawns in a little more oil for 4–5 minutes. Toss the chicken pieces, pak choi and prawns together and either serve with the prawn toasts on one big plate in the middle of the table, or divide up on to separate plates. Drizzle generously with the dressing.

SMOKED HAM HOCK, CELERIAC, APPLE AND ENDIVE SALAD

This is a fantastic recipe that will give you a beautiful cooking liquor which you must not throw away! It's very important to make the best use of everything in the kitchen, so once you have finished with the liquor you can either freeze it for another day or make it into the most delicious pea and ham soup, or cabbage and bacon soup with potatoes. Boiling cheap cuts of meat is such a good way of cooking them, as they become very tender. Just remember to keep topping the pan up with water and to cover it while cooking, otherwise the liquid will reduce down and become too salty. The dressing I've given here is best used while the meat is warm, otherwise it will solidify. So once you've pulled your bits of meat apart, put them back into the cooking liquor to keep them warm until you're ready to serve. Any leftovers are great for sandwiches.

SERVES 4
1kg smoked ham hock / 1 carrot, peeled and chopped / 1 onion, peeled and chopped / 1 leek, trimmed and chopped / 1 bay leaf / 1 sprig of fresh thyme / 1 clove of garlic, peeled / 6 white peppercorns / ½ a celeriac / 2 Granny Smith apples / 3 large endives (chicory) / a handful of mixed fresh herbs (flat-leaf parsley, chives and coriander), chopped

MUSTARD AND HONEY DRESSING
285ml classic vinaigrette (see page 217) / 1 tablespoon grain mustard / 2 tablespoons runny honey

Soak the ham hock for 2 hours in cold water. After soaking, place it in a pan deep enough to be able to cover it with fresh water. Add the carrot, onion, leek, bay leaf, thyme, garlic and white peppercorns. Bring to the boil, skim, and simmer for approximately 2 hours until the meat is tender and falling from the bone. Let the hock cool in the cooking liquor and then pull the meat from the skin in good-sized chunks. Place these pieces of meat back into the cooking liquor until ready to serve.

Mix together the dressing ingredients. Peel the celeriac and cut it into fine batons. Cut the apples into quarters, then slice lengthways on a mandolin to give you fine quarter-circle slices. Pull apart the leaves from the endives. Mix all the ingredients with the chunks of ham, glaze with the dressing, toss together and serve in shallow bowls. Finish with a sprinkling of herbs and serve with crusty rolls and a glass of Chardonnay.

CRISPY DUCK SALAD

With roast duck, you often find that only the breast meat is eaten. This is a fantastic way to use the legs so they don't go to waste. It's a really lovely starter – the duck meat is great with the fresh, peppery watercress. This is the recipe that I put on the menu at the Glass House to replace the awful duck balls that they served me.

SERVES 4
6 duck legs / 2 star anise / ½ a bulb of garlic / 20g fresh ginger, roughly chopped / a small bunch of fresh coriander, leaves picked, stalks kept / vegetable oil for deep frying / 2 bunches of watercress, washed and picked / ½ a white radish, peeled then shaved into ribbons / 30g beansprouts / a bunch of spring onions, sliced / 2 tablespoons toasted sesame seeds

SAUCE
4 tablespoons tomato ketchup / 100ml honey, soy and sesame dressing (see page 219)

Put the duck legs, star anise, garlic and ginger into a large pan. Add the coriander stalks and cover with water. Bring to the boil, then turn the heat down and simmer gently for about 45 minutes until tender. Drain and then leave the meat to cool. When the duck legs have cooled enough to handle them, strip the meat away from the bone – it should come away easily – removing the skin and leaving a little of the fat on the meat. Cut into even-sized strips about 1cm thick.

Mix the sauce ingredients together. Heat the oil to 180°C/350°C in a deep heavy-bottomed pan or a deep fat fryer and fry the strips of duck until crisp. When done, mix the duck into the sauce until each piece is well coated. Finally mix all the salad ingredients with the duck, add the sesame seeds, and toss well just before serving.

CRAB AND GINGER SALAD WITH BABY GEM, LEMON CONFIT AND FENNEL SHAVINGS

Crab is very under-used in this country as people often feel intimidated by it. I don't much use brown crab but when I do I thicken it with mayonnaise so it becomes a beautiful paste and serve it smeared on bruschetta. The king of the crab world is the white crab — it has an amazing flavour. It's also pretty good when you buy the meat ready-picked. But the most flavoursome crabs in the world are spider crabs — unfortunately they are not used in Britain all that much, as the preparation, picking all the meat out from the legs, is seen as too lengthy.

The idea of this salad is to show you a light, fragrant and exciting way to eat crab. The ginger and lemon confit give it a lift. At the Boxwood Café we serve it with passion fruit for the same reason. Here I've also used apple and fennel — very delicate flavours which are not too rich for the palate. Fennel is often sliced too thickly in restaurants, which makes it harder to digest. Here I've used a mandolin and would suggest you do the same — try to get used to using one of these, as they give you really thin slices and it's easy to do.

SERVES 4

2 Granny Smith apples, cored and diced / a small bunch of fresh chives or coriander, chopped / 250g fresh, picked white crabmeat / 1 small red chilli, deseeded and finely chopped / zest of 1 lemon / 10g grated ginger / 50ml mayonnaise (see page 228) / 2 baby gem lettuces, divided into leaves / classic vinaigrette (see page 217) / 8–10 slices of lemon confit (see page 235) / 1 bulb of fennel, finely sliced and soaked in iced water / salt and freshly ground black pepper / fresh coriander leaves

Mix the apples, herbs, crabmeat, chilli, lemon zest, ginger and mayonnaise in a bowl. Drizzle the baby gem leaves with the vinaigrette, toss together and lay on a chilled plate. Mix the lemon confit with the fennel shavings, season, and scatter this over the gem lettuce, leaving a well in the centre. Spoon the crabmeat into the centre of the salad and sprinkle a few leaves of coriander over the top.

GRILLED VEGETABLE SALAD MARINATED IN LEMON AND BASIL OIL

This salad can be made with various different vegetables, so have a go at putting together a selection of your own. Celeriac is a great one to use — usually easier to grill if you slice it into thick flat pieces. Green tomatoes are absolutely delicious when grilled like this, or you can use big red beef tomatoes with chopped rosemary. Potatoes are really nice, parboiled first, drizzled with some olive oil, then seasoned with thyme flowers — the ultimate sauté potatoes! Sweet potato is also good like this and reminds me of my days working in the Caribbean. Sweetcorn (on the cob), part-cooked in butter and then grilled, is absolutely lovely, as are baby artichokes.

SERVES 4
1 bunch of asparagus, peeled and blanched / 2 large courgettes, cut into 1cm thick diagonal slices / 1 small aubergine, cut into 1cm slices / 2 red peppers, skinned and quartered / 2 large fennel, quartered / 2 medium-sized red onions, peeled and quartered / 2 cloves of garlic, lightly crushed / lemon and basil infused olive oil (see page 221) / 1 tablespoon balsamic vinegar / rock salt / ground coriander

On a red-hot chargrill pan, or directly on your barbecue, cook all the vegetables until they have just a little bite left. Place in a deep dish and scatter the garlic on top. Drizzle the oil over the warm vegetables, followed by the balsamic vinegar. Mix well so that every-thing is generously glazed with the oil. Sprinkle with rock salt and ground coriander, then cover with clingfilm and marinate for an hour before serving. These vegetables are amazing when eaten cold as a salad, or warm with lamb or beef.

BEING A WAITER

I'm really fortunate to have the James Bond of maître d's working for me at Royal Hospital Road. Jean-Claude is a restaurant owner's dream. We met when we were both working at Le Gavroche, and his level of tolerance with customers really impressed me. He has that incredible knack of making every single diner feel welcome, and he knows exactly how much attention he should pay each table. He can recommend and help you choose the right dish, whether it's a dainty plate of scallops for Madame or a braised pig cheek for Monsieur.

If you're having a quiet lunch with a lover, Jean-Claude will be discreet but charming; if it's a business dinner, he'll be attentive without making an impression; and if it's three girls on a night out, then he'll flirt and flatter as any true Frenchman would. He has a remarkable sense of humour and the best smile in the business.

I absolutely insist that all my new chefs take a turn at being a waiter before they start in the kitchen. It makes them realize how demanding a job it is and helps them develop respect for the restaurant staff. As a chef in the kitchen, there are places to hide, to let off steam, but in the dining room the waiters are on show the whole time. Every table, from the first to the last, must have the same standard of service.

When I was filming the series I couldn't believe how miserable a lot of the waiting staff were. So few of them seemed to really enjoy their job. I wouldn't have been happy with them emptying the kitchen bins, let alone serving me a meal. And when they're leaning over you with dog breath and greasy hair and there's filth under their fingernails, it really puts you off your food.

A waiter must be presentable, diplomatic, unbiased and the most fantastic listener — the last thing a customer wants to hear is the waiter's problems. That's what makes Jean-Claude so special — he cares about every single person who walks through the door.

things on toast

'There are so many amazing varieties of bread, and that was the inspiration behind this whole chapter'

The sandwich menu at the Glass House was an embarrassment. It just didn't fit in with the rest of the food they were serving there. The BLT was made with dry, overcooked bacon and re-heated bread. It's a classy restaurant and they really let themselves down with their lunchtime sandwich menu.

So instead I showed them how to make 'things on toast' — something we do well at the Boxwood Café. Even the kitchen porter, who had a fish phobia, thought the mackerel on toast was one of the best things he'd ever eaten. In fact he had three of them one day for his lunch! There are other really great, simple recipes here, like my favourite, lobster roll.

GRILLED SARDINES AND CHUNKY PROVENÇAL TOMATO SAUCE ON TOASTED POILANE BREAD

In Britain, sardines are regarded as the poor man's fish. Yet in places like Roses, which is a town two hours outside Barcelona, sardines caught locally are the absolute king fish, the jewel in the crown. The nice thing about cooking and eating sardines (grill them, as they are oily) is that everything is self-contained. They have a very high protein value, so I like to eat them around running time — whether I'm training for a marathon or just out jogging. We serve sardines at the Boxwood Café and it's a nice way of eating something which has maybe been a bit forgotten about. Don't waste your time trying to pick all the bones out — they will be so soft when cooked that they will just disintegrate.

SERVES 1
2–3 sardine fillets / olive oil / rock salt and freshly ground black pepper / 1 large thick slice of pain poilane or other sourdough bread / 1½ cloves of garlic, 1 crushed, ½ chopped / a pinch of fresh thyme / 1 large shallot, finely chopped / 10–12 cherry tomatoes / 2–3 fresh basil leaves

Lay the sardines skin side up on a baking tray and drizzle with olive oil. Sprinkle with rock salt and grill until the skin goes slightly crisp. Meanwhile, rub the bread with the crushed garlic and a little oil, then sprinkle over the thyme leaves and a little rock salt. Toast slowly on both sides so the bread becomes crisp.

In a large sauté pan cook the shallots and chopped garlic in 2 tablespoons of olive oil until soft. Halve the cherry tomatoes, add to the pan, and continue to cook over a high heat so that they break down slightly. Tear the basil leaves into the pan and remove from the heat. Place the hot tomato sauce directly on the crisp toast and top with the sardines. Finish with some freshly ground black pepper.

GRILLED FLAT MUSHROOMS AND PANCETTA ON TOASTED BRIOCHE WITH WELSH RAREBIT

Brioche is the ballerina of breads – light, subtle, but with an acquired taste (it's usually served with pâté, which I cringe at). You can get hold of flat-capped field mushrooms anywhere, and they are full of flavour. When you mix them with pancetta, cheese and mustard, it's like a posh cheese on toast. It's a quick and easy snack with a wonderful creamy topping and amazing field mushrooms underneath. Absolutely delicious.

SERVES 1

3–4 flat mushrooms, peeled and trimmed / olive oil / 4–5 slices good smoked pancetta / 1 slice of large brioche, toasted / 25g grated strong Cheddar cheese / 1 tablespoon English mustard / 4–5 dashes of Worcestershire sauce / 2 small egg yolks / 2 tablespoons whipped cream / sea salt and freshly ground black pepper

Fry the mushrooms in olive oil until cooked, and drain on some kitchen paper. Grill the pancetta until crisp. Lay the mushrooms neatly on the toasted brioche, with the pancetta on top. Mix together the cheese, mustard, Worcestershire sauce and egg yolks and then fold in the cream. Season well and spoon gently over the pancetta. Place under a very hot grill until golden and bubbling.

GRILLED PLUM TOMATOES WITH BABY MOZZARELLA, BASIL AND OLIVE OIL

Growing up in a large family with limited money, tomatoes on toast was something we always had on a Sunday night before bathtime and bed. I enjoy reminiscing about having comfort food like this round the table. This recipe is based on our family original, but is slightly more sophisticated with an updated twist using mozzarella (much to my mother's annoyance!). Just like a mini pizza.

Ciabatta bread is lovely toasted like this with a drizzle of olive oil. It's a great base to use as it doesn't go soggy. And wilt some extra basil over the mozzarella when grilled — it will be so fragrant.

SERVES 1

1 slice of ciabatta / 1 tablespoon black olive paste / 3 large fresh basil leaves, plus extra for garnish / 1 plum tomato, skinned and sliced / rock salt and freshly ground black pepper / 2–3 baby mozzarella cheeses (or ½ a large one) / olive oil / a sprig of thyme

Toast the ciabatta on both sides. Spread the black olive paste over one side and lay the basil leaves on top. Cut the tomato into about 6 or 7 slices and lay these over the basil. Season with salt and pepper, then tear the mozzarella over the tomatoes and drizzle with olive oil. Place under a very hot grill until the cheese is melted and glazed. Garnish with basil leaves and thyme flowers.

LOBSTER ROLL

I first came across the idea of a lobster roll at the Gramercy Tavern in New York, where the meat was bound together by a dressing. It's the perfect sandwich – pure decadence, but presented in a hot-dog style and made with leftover trimmings, and that's what I love about it. If you can't get lobster you can use crevettes or crayfish instead.

SERVES 1
1 x 500g Scottish lobster / 2 tablespoons mayonnaise (see page 228) / 1 tablespoon tomato ketchup / a dash of Worcestershire or Tabasco sauce / 2 spring onions, sliced / a pinch of chopped gherkin / 1 large red pepper, diced / 1 small soft baguette / 2–3 leaves of iceberg lettuce, finely shredded

Kill the lobster and remove the claws and tail (see page 240). Plunge these into a large pan of boiling water, then reduce the heat and simmer the claws for 9 minutes and the tail for 7 minutes. Make sure you don't boil it, though, or the meat will become tough. Drain, put to one side and allow to cool.

Remove the meat from the lobster and chop into bite-sized chunks. Mix the mayonnaise, ketchup, Worcestershire or Tabasco sauce, spring onions, gherkin and pepper together to form a Thousand Island dressing, then add the lobster meat and mix well. Cut the roll lengthways down the centre and open it out like a hot-dog roll. Place the lettuce leaves on the roll and spoon plenty of the lobster filling on top so it oozes out and runs down the sides!

ROASTED SUCKLING PIG WITH COLESLAW AND ROCKET ON GRANARY

The Glass House needed a classic weekend lunch menu, and I suggested that they should do a whole roast suckling pig and keep any leftovers to make sandwiches on the Monday – gorgeous served on an open roll or a slice of granary (sourdough would be brilliant as well), topped with peppery coleslaw and a touch of rocket. A great lunch starter, or even a main course, as they are quite substantial servings.

SERVES 1 (WITH PLENTY FOR LEFTOVERS)
1 small loin of suckling pig, boned, or pork belly / sea salt and freshly ground black pepper / zest of 1 lemon / 1 bunch of fresh sage, leaves picked / 1 carrot, grated / ¼ of a white cabbage, finely shredded / 1 small red onion, sliced / mayonnaise (see page 228) / granary bread / a small handful of baby rocket / olive oil

Preheat the oven to 200°C/400°F/gas 6. Lay the suckling pig or pork belly out flat and season it well. Rub with the lemon zest and spread with the sage leaves. Roll and tie the meat and roast in the oven for 25–30 minutes until the skin is crisp. Remove from the oven and leave to cool, then wrap it in clingfilm and refrigerate for 1 hour.

Meanwhile, mix the carrot, cabbage and onion with the mayonnaise to make your coleslaw and season to taste. Toast a thick slice of granary bread and spoon over a generous amount of coleslaw, sprinkled with a few rocket leaves. Cut yourself 3–4 slices of meat, season, drizzle with a little olive oil, and place over the coleslaw and rocket.

MACKEREL ON TOAST WITH A WARM POTATO SALAD

Mackerel really is the most underrated fish in the sea today, and yet it's full of flavour. It was an instant hit as soon as it went on the menu at the Glass House with a warm Charlotte potato salad, vibrant spring onions and a touch of lemon juice with crème fraîche. Don't be scared to keep the mackerel pink. When I cooked it I made inserts in the skin to stop the fish curling up, so do try this. You can always ask your fishmonger to fillet and bone it for you. A very cheap but very exciting way of making an open toasted sandwich.

SERVES 1
2–3 Charlotte potatoes / 2 spring onions, finely sliced / a small bunch of fresh chives, finely chopped / 1 tablespoon lemon juice / 1 tablespoon crème fraîche / sea salt and freshly ground black pepper / ½ a crusty roll, toasted / 1 small mackerel, filleted and boned / olive oil

With their skins left on, gently poach the potatoes in salted water until soft. When cool enough to handle, cut into cubes. Mix with the spring onions, chives and lemon juice and bind with the crème fraîche. Season with salt and pepper and spread generously on to the toasted roll.

Meanwhile, in a hot non-stick pan, sauté the mackerel in olive oil, skin side down, until crisp. Turn over and cook the underside for a few minutes. Remove from the pan and place on to the potato salad. Eat while still warm.

SMOKED SALMON AND CREAM CHEESE CROQUE MONSIEUR

The French are very good at naming things with a twist. Croque monsieur is basically cheese on toast, so the idea behind this was to take it to another level by using smoked salmon — you can even add caviar if you like. It gives another dimension to the classic French sandwich.

SERVES 1
2 slices of square brioche / 50g cream cheese / a very small bunch of fresh chives, chopped / sea salt and freshly ground black pepper / juice of ¼ of a lemon / 2 slices of Gruyère cheese / 4 good slices of smoked salmon / 10g caviar (optional)

Toast one side of the brioche slices. Mix the cream cheese and chives together and season with black pepper and lemon juice. Spread half the cream cheese on the toasted side of the bread, and cover with two slices of smoked salmon. Then lay a piece of Gruyère on top, followed by a couple more salmon slices. Spread the remaining cream cheese on top of the salmon and spoon over a little caviar, if using. Press the two halves gently together and toast the untoasted sides. Remove the crusts with a sharp knife and then cut in half diagonally.

Running a successful restaurant is all about making a good impression as soon as the customers walk through the door. What's the first thing you're given to eat when you sit down at the table? The bread. That sets the tone. If the meal starts off on a high, it gets the customer excited about what's to come. And if you don't have the resources to bake bread, then find the best local baker you can. At the Walnut Tree the waiter also doubled up as baker and odd-job man. The bread he made every morning was exquisite — no fancy twists and rolls, just good simple rustic loaves freshly sliced to order.

THE TABLE TRICK

If, like most of the places I visited, your restaurant's half empty from Monday to Thursday, then a great trick is to remove one third of the tables to give the impression the dining room's constantly full. It creates intimacy, and makes the customer feel they've come to the hottest spot in town. You can pretty much guarantee they'll book again.

CREATING AN AMBIENCE

Lighting should be adjusted three or four times a day to create the right atmosphere, whether you're a Michelin-starred restaurant or a gastropub. It's no good having a brightly lit dining room at eight in the evening when everyone's settling in for an intimate dinner. And remember, ladies like to glow but they don't like to be in the spotlight.

ACOUSTICS

If your restaurant has wooden floors and no carpet you have to create softness on the walls — something to soak up the hubbub. You want to be able to hear the people at your table, not the loud-mouthed city boy who's bragging about his latest investment deal on the other side of the room.

SITTING COMFORTABLY

If the chairs are uncomfortable the guests won't stay around. Even if you can't afford the best-upholstered seating, a simple cushion will do the trick, because the longer the customers are in the restaurant, the more money they'll spend. And the more they spend, the more successful the business.

vegetarian

'I was misquoted a few years ago, so I want to set the record straight: I absolutely love vegetarians, adore them, and enjoy eating vegetarian food myself!'

Vegetarian food is a refreshing break from eating meat and fish from time to time. My secret for vegetarians is, whenever you're going out to eat, always ring the restaurant beforehand to let them know you are vegetarian. Chefs love being put to the test. We have vegetarian menus in all my restaurants, because I get so pissed off when I see chefs being lazy with vegetarian food. When they go out with a herb risotto or herb omelette or a tomato and basil salad it's wrong. Absolutely wrong. There should be an elaborate little tian of marinated tomatoes, or beautiful stuffed courgette flowers, or wonderful braised lentils with Swiss chard, turnips and parsley ravioli like we have on the menu at the Boxwood Café. That's the way to treat vegetarians.

In a good restaurant, you should make your vegetarian food just as carefully as you would if you were cooking for the à la carte menu. The dishes have to be exciting. I do think some chefs in this country tend to be lazy with vegetarian dishes because they have that old chef syndrome of 'I can't be bothered', and it's unfair, because after all we're charging the same prices. At my restaurant in Chelsea we have an eight-course tasting menu, and alongside it we run an eight-course tasting menu for vegetarians.

The recipes in this chapter are just lovely, and can be enjoyed by everyone. The baked pumpkin gives you a really nice autumnal feel and it makes a wonderful starter. With the penne recipe, the real flavour lies in the juice from the cherry and vine tomatoes. The tomato, onion and potato gratin is the most amazing dish on its own — a substantial, rich winter warmer.

GORGONZOLA RISOTTO WITH PEAS AND BROAD BEANS

When you cook risotto at home you can do the whole thing in one go from start to finish because you have plenty of time to stir it — in my restaurants we have to blanch the rice first and then bring it all together later on. It's a nice way of speeding up the process — the rice just goes back into the pan with the stock and quickly starts to become workable. However, for this recipe we will cook the rice in the stock as usual. The secret is never to flood the risotto with liquid, otherwise the rice becomes overcooked, with a horrible furry exterior.

You can flavour risottos in so many ways. The creamy Gorgonzola cheese in this recipe is naturally salty, along with the Parmesan, so all you really need to finish it off is a knob of butter, which gives a nice, smooth, velvety texture. To cut back on the richness of the cheese I've added peas and broad beans. Asparagus would also work well.

SERVES 4

100g butter, diced / 1 onion, peeled and finely chopped / 400g Arborio or other risotto rice / 1 litre vegetable stock / 2 tablespoons white wine / 150g petits pois, cooked / 150g shelled broad beans, cooked / 50g Parmesan cheese, grated, plus Parmesan shavings for serving / 75g Gorgonzola cheese, diced / sea salt and freshly ground black pepper / a small handful of rocket

Melt 50g of the butter in a large pan. Add the onion and cook until soft and translucent. Add the rice and stir into the onion, coating all the grains. Slowly add the hot stock, a ladleful at a time, waiting until each ladleful has been absorbed by the rice before adding the next and stirring often. After 20 minutes the rice should be cooked — it should be quite moist and relaxed, with a very slight bite. At this point, add the wine, peas and broad beans and stir in the remaining butter and the graated Parmesan. Remove from the heat and fold in the diced Gorgonzola. Check the seasoning and serve at once, garnished with some rocket leaves and Parmesan shavings.

VINAIGRETTE OF LEEKS WITH PINK GRAPEFRUIT HOLLANDAISE

A great vegetarian dish, especially when livened up a bit with zesty pink grapefruit hollandaise. With leeks there seems to be a fascination for 'baby' ones looking better on the plate, so the large ones are now, sadly, used more in stocks and soups. So I wanted to give you a great way of cooking the larger ones. When you prepare them, all you have to do is remove the outer layer, as this is the stringy bit — you can unravel it like a cigar. But don't throw it away, as you can still use it to make stocks and soups.

SERVES 4
8 large leeks, peeled and trimmed / sea salt and freshly ground black pepper / 100g butter, diced / 2 cloves of garlic, quartered / ½ a small bunch of fresh thyme / classic vinaigrette (see page 217) / pink grapefruit hollandaise (see page 229) / a few sprigs of fresh chervil

Preheat the oven to 180°C/350°F/gas 4. Place the leeks in the sink under running water and wash well, ensuring all dirt has been removed. Lay them in an ovenproof dish, approximately 5cm deep, which holds the leeks tightly together. Season well and pour over the 200ml of water so that the leeks are just covered. Dot the butter over and add the garlic and thyme to the tray. Cover the tray with foil, and cook in the preheated oven for 20–25 minutes. The leeks should braise slowly in their own juices, but check them every so often during cooking — if they get too dry, just add a spoonful or two of water.

When cooked, the leeks should be soft and glazed but still whole. Remove to the fridge to cool. When totally cold, slice each leek into three pieces and glaze with the vinaigrette. To serve, arrange six pieces of leek per person on a plate and coat with the pink grapefruit hollandaise. Garnish with a few sprigs of chervil.

BAKED PUMPKIN

This is a great way to use awkwardly shaped pumpkins — the ones you can't roast or bake whole. The recipe also works well with butternut squash. Cooking it like this really helps to bring out the flavour of pumpkin and it's just lovely with the soothing, melting-textured gratinate. I would serve this with a salad.

SERVES 4
1kg ripe pumpkin (unpeeled weight) / sea salt and freshly ground black pepper / 5-6 tablespoons olive oil / 1 tablespoon pumpkin oil (if unavailable, use olive oil) / 150g unsweetened brioche, crusts removed / 1 shallot, finely chopped / a sprig of fresh thyme, leaves picked and finely chopped / 2–3 sprigs of fresh coriander, finely chopped / 1 teaspoon fresh chives, finely chopped / 20g Parmesan cheese, grated / 20g Gruyère cheese, grated

Peel and halve the pumpkin and remove any seeds and stringy membranes. Slice the pumpkin halves into 1cm thick wedges and season with salt and pepper. Heat 3–4 tablespoons of olive oil in a frying pan and sauté the pumpkin for about 6 minutes, until caramelized and softened slightly. Transfer to an ovenproof dish and drizzle with the pumpkin oil.

Blitz the brioche in a food processor until you have fine crumbs, then tip them into a bowl. Sauté the shallot in 1 tablespoon of olive oil until soft, without colouring it, then add to the brioche crumbs with the herbs, Parmesan and Gruyère. Mix well, adding more olive oil to moisten as necessary. You don't want the mixture to be dry. Sprinkle over the pumpkin slices and press down lightly. Place in the oven, preheated to 220°C/425°F/gas 7, for a maximum of 5 minutes, or under a hot grill, until the topping is crispy and golden.

TWICE BAKED CHEESE SOUFFLÉS

This recipe dispels any myths that soufflés are hard to make. They can be very easy — just make sure you have non-stick dishes. Don't even attempt it without, or your work will become twice as hard. And remember that you must try not to open the oven door while the soufflés are cooking. If you feel you have to check on their progress, then open the door, but don't let it slam shut as this will have an impact on the temperature. Try not to be too clever too soon when it comes to soufflés. Start off with a basic recipe like this one, and once you've cracked it you can afford to be a bit more flamboyant with your flavours and textures.

Twice baking is your safety net if you're doing soufflés for a dinner party — so you don't have any embarrassment whatsoever when you come to serve them! I've been in so many situations where I've sat there and seen soufflés not work. This way is fail-proof and will give you guaranteed success at the table!

MAKES 8 SOUFFLÉS
melted butter for dishes / 425ml milk / a grating of nutmeg / a 30g piece of onion, peeled / 85g butter / 85g flour / 225g mature Cheddar cheese, finely grated, plus extra for serving / 6 eggs, separated / 1 tablespoon English mustard / 300ml double cream, plus extra for brushing / finely chopped flat-leaf parsley

Preheat the oven to 170°C/325°F/gas 3. Butter eight small non-stick baking dishes, cups or mugs and prepare a bain-marie (see page 244), which will be used to cook the soufflés in the oven. Warm the milk in a saucepan, add the nutmeg and onion, and leave to infuse for 10–15 minutes. Melt the butter in a second saucepan and add the flour, cooking gently for 2 minutes without colouring. Remove the onion from the milk and slowly add the milk to the pan, a third at a time, stirring continuously. When all the milk has been added, continue to stir over the heat for 1 minute more. Remove the pan from the heat and add the cheese, stirring until it is fully melted. Then add the egg yolks and mustard. Transfer the mixture to a large clean bowl. Stiffly whip the egg whites in a separate bowl and fold in. Fill your buttered baking dishes two-thirds full with the mixture, giving you enough room for the soufflés to rise, stand them in the bain-marie, and cook in the preheated oven for 25–30 minutes.

Remove the dishes from the bain-marie and leave to cool for 1 hour. Just before you are ready to serve, turn the oven up to 240°C/475°F/gas 9. Run a knife round the inside of each baking dish to loosen the soufflés. Remove them from the dishes and place them upside down in separate ovenproof serving dishes. Brush the sides with cream and place a tablespoonful of grated cheese on top. Add 2 tablespoons of cream to each dish then cook in the oven for approximately 7 minutes until golden brown and bubbling.

PUFF PASTRY PIZZA

This is an incredibly easy way to make a pizza. The salad of tomatoes on page 76 would be a good accompaniment. The best thing about this pizza is that the base is puff pastry instead of a yeast dough, so it's lovely and crisp. It's also a great one to cook when trying to wean your children off synthetic pizzas. When making your own pizzas you're in complete control because you can choose the toppings you want – Dolcelatte, mascarpone, tomatoes or olives, even things like anchovies, the lovely black ham called 'pata negra' or goat's cheese. When considering what to top your pizza with, think of the weight underneath it and the water content of the topping ingredients, as the worst thing is a soggy pizza base. Think of things on top that don't need any cooking rather than raw ingredients. I've suggested seasoning with thyme, but do try using chervil, parsley or basil.

SERVES 4
flour / 250g puff pastry / 50g butter / 250g baby spinach, washed / sea salt and freshly ground black pepper / a grating of nutmeg / 1 tablespoon mascarpone cheese / 55g Parmesan cheese, grated, plus a little extra to finish / 12 cherry tomatoes, halved / 10 black olives, pitted and halved / 15 fresh anchovy fillets / 100g Dolcelatte cheese / 100g goat's cheese/ a sprig of fresh thyme, leaves picked / 1 egg yolk, beaten

Preheat the oven to 180°C/350°F/gas 4. Lightly dust a work surface with flour and roll out the puff pastry until you have a rough rectangle 25 x 15cm – thin, but not so thin that it's see-through. Put it in the fridge to rest for 5 minutes, then, using the back of a knife, lightly score around the pastry about 1cm from the edge, to create a lip or rim. Place on a piece of greaseproof paper on a baking tray.

Meanwhile, melt a knob of butter and sauté the spinach until wilted, seasoning it with salt, pepper and nutmeg. Drain on kitchen paper and refrigerate until well chilled. Using a clean cloth, squeeze out any excess moisture from the spinach, then roughly chop it. Put it into a bowl and add the mascarpone and half the Parmesan. Mix well, and check the seasoning. Spoon this mixture on to the middle of the puff pastry base, leaving the rim clear. Scatter the cherry tomatoes over the top, then do the same with the olives. Lay the anchovies over. Break up the Dolcelatte and goat's cheese and scatter these over the top. To finish, sprinkle with the remaining Parmesan and the thyme leaves, and season with some more pepper. Using a pastry brush, brush the egg yolk round the lip to give a nice glazed finish. Bake the pizza in the preheated oven for about 20 minutes, or until the pastry has risen and turned golden and the base is crisp.

PENNE WITH CHERRY TOMATO SAUCE

This is my Saturday family dish, because Sunday is my morning for a two-and-a-half-hour run and I try to load up on carbos the day before. It's also a good one for the kids. I tend to use the 'disguise' method to try to get them off sweet things, and this recipe is a good one for that reason. I sneak some basil or parsley into the tomatoes to stop them being so sweet. Penne is an easy pasta for kids to eat and it's less messy than spaghetti, which means more in their mouths and less on the floor!

SERVES 4

100g unsalted butter / 4 cloves of garlic, peeled and crushed / 1kg cherry tomatoes, halved / sea salt and freshly ground black pepper / a bunch of fresh basil, leaves picked / 400g penne pasta / 120g Parmesan cheese, grated, plus Parmesan shavings for serving

Melt half the butter in a large pan and fry the garlic until it colours lightly. Add the tomatoes and a good pinch of salt and simmer for about 15 minutes. Add the basil leaves, reserving a few small ones, and remove from the heat. Meanwhile, cook the penne in a large pan of boiling water until al dente. Drain, season and mix in the Parmesan and remaining butter. Then stir in the tomato sauce. Serve garnished with fresh Parmesan shavings and the reserved basil leaves.

TOMATO, ONION AND POTATO GRATIN

When you have friends round there is usually a vegetarian lurking somewhere, and this is a perfect dish to make for them. It's also really good served with roast chicken or a classic Sunday roast, and it can be made in advance and then heated up just before serving. Thyme flowers are a nice seasonal twist, and good Italian tomatoes really make this dish. So, next time a vegetarian unexpectedly pops up, this one's for them.

SERVES 4

450g onions, peeled / 4 tablespoons olive oil / sea salt and freshly ground black pepper / 700g potatoes, peeled and thinly sliced / 2 sprigs of fresh thyme, leaves picked / 6 juniper berries, crushed / butter, for greasing dish / 1 bay leaf / 450g plum tomatoes, skinned and sliced thinly

Preheat the oven to 170°C/325°F/gas 3. Slice the onions thinly and cook gently in 2 tablespoons of olive oil until caramelized. Season, then remove to some kitchen paper to drain. Put the potatoes, thyme, juniper berries and remaining oil in a bowl, season and mix well. Get yourself an oval gratin dish, butter it well, then layer the potatoes, onions and tomatoes in that order, until all the ingredients have been used up, making sure you finish with a layer of potatoes. Tuck in the bay leaf. Sprinkle on 2 tablespoons of water. Bake in the oven for about an hour until crunchy and golden on top and soft inside.

BRAISED BELGIAN ENDIVE

I enjoy eating endives in a salad, but they have far more flavour when roasted in the oven or braised, as they are here with capers, garlic and chilli. The endives take on a sweet and sour flavour and almost caramelize in their own juices very slowly. I like this type of rustic approach – and I don't mind the bitterness of endive either, but you can sprinkle them with a little caster sugar and lemon juice if you like, as this counteracts the bitterness. Endive is a dainty and delicate vegetable, so it's much better with fish than with meat – try it alongside roast cod or salmon.

SERVES 4
2 cloves of garlic / 1 tablespoon small capers / ½ a fresh red chilli, finely chopped / 4 tablespoons olive oil / 4 Belgian endives / juice of ½ a lemon / sea salt and freshly ground black pepper

Put the garlic, capers, chilli and olive oil into a frying pan over a gentle heat and cook for 1 minute. Add the endives and about 300ml of water. Cover with a piece of buttered greaseproof paper and cook slowly for about 30 minutes until the endives are tender. Squeeze over the lemon juice, season and serve.

SALAD OF TOMATOES WITH AUBERGINE CAVIAR AND CORIANDER CRESS

This is a lovely way to eat tomatoes, especially the flavoursome vine tomatoes, or the often under-valued beef tomatoes. For this recipe it is best to use a selection of different varieties, such as red cherry, cherry plum, vine, green beef, Dutch orange plum, yellow cherry or rustic plum. Whenever we have tomatoes at home, I leave them out on the side, as they won't ripen if you keep them in the fridge. They also tend to plump up more if you don't chill them. I treat them like avocados, as they tend to bruise easily. Coriander cress is baby coriander seedlings – if not available, use coriander leaves or mustard and cress.

SERVES 4

1 large aubergine / 1 clove of garlic, peeled and sliced / rock salt / olive oil / a sprig of fresh rosemary / sea salt and freshly ground black pepper / 250g mixed tomatoes per serving / classic vinaigrette (see page 217) / 1 punnet of coriander cress, or a small handful of coriander leaves / 4 small shallots, sliced into fine rings / a small handful of rocket

Preheat the oven to 220°C/425°F/gas 7. Cut the aubergine in half lengthways and score the flesh. Scatter the garlic over the scored sides of the aubergine, then sprinkle with rock salt. Drizzle a little olive oil over and sandwich the two halves together, with the sprig of rosemary between. Wrap tightly in foil and bake in the preheated oven for 45 minutes, then reduce the heat to 110°C/225°F/gas ¼ and bake for a further 25 minutes. Unwrap the aubergine, remove the rosemary, and scrape the aubergine flesh and garlic into a bowl. Stir until pulpy, then transfer to a pan and cook over a high heat until any liquid has evaporated and the mixture has thickened. Check the seasoning and leave to cool.

Slice all the tomatoes neatly and season. Glaze with some classic vinaigrette and leave to steep for about 5 minutes. To serve, either spoon the aubergine caviar into the middle of four plates, or have a go at taking two large dessertspoons and shaping scoops of the caviar into quenelles. Put one on each plate, then place the tomatoes around the outside and sprinkle with your coriander cress or coriander leaves. Scatter over the shallot rings and a few small leaves of rocket.

BAKED ASPARAGUS AND PARMESAN LOAF

This is my version of a modern-day quiche – it has cream, eggs and nutmeg in it, and if you want to jazz it up further you can use half green and half white asparagus. The custard is used as a packing agent to keep it all together, and, if you like, a handful of flat-leaf parsley blitzed in will colour it green, which finishes it off nicely. Don't be scared to put fresh peas and broad beans in there too, as this will give it a lovely flavour. If you're using the small thin pencil asparagus, don't peel it, but if the spears are large then do.

SERVES 4

1kg fresh asparagus, trimmed / 75g butter / 1 large loaf of white bread, sliced, crusts removed / 3 eggs, beaten / 300ml double cream / 100g Parmesan cheese, grated / sea salt and freshly ground black pepper / a grating of nutmeg

Preheat the oven to 200°C/400°F/gas 6. Cook the asparagus in boiling salted water for about 7–8 minutes and refresh under cold water. Grease a 22cm loaf tin with a little of the butter, then line it with bread slices, leaving a few for covering the top. Overlap them a little and gently press them down to make sure the bread lines the tin snugly. Mix the eggs and cream together, add the Parmesan, and season with salt, pepper and nutmeg.

Now place half the asparagus in the tin and season. Pour over half the egg mixture and repeat, layering the asparagus and egg mixture again. Butter the remaining bread and lay on top, buttered side up. Bake in the preheated oven for approximately 45 minutes until golden, then turn out of the tin and let it cool slightly before carefully cutting it into slices.

PEPPERS BRAISED IN RED WINE

This is a lovely starter with a northern Spanish influence. The great news is that you don't have to go through the laborious task of peeling the peppers, because if you do you will take a lot of their flavour and goodness away. Rosé wine also works well if you don't have red. The end result is almost like a pepper and tomato compote, and I like to eat it at room temperature or warm. A nice way to serve this is to fill some large crisp baby gem lettuce leaves with the peppers and accompany them with some grilled sourdough bread, drizzled with olive oil and sprinkled with rock salt.

SERVES 4

4 tablespoons olive oil / 4 cloves of garlic, peeled and sliced / 25g sliced red shallots / 400g cherry tomatoes, halved / sea salt and freshly ground black pepper / 4 large red peppers, halved and deseeded / 4 large yellow peppers, halved and deseeded / 300ml red wine / a small bunch of fresh basil, leaves picked / olive oil to finish

Heat 2 tablespoons of olive oil in a large pan and fry the garlic and shallots until soft. Add the tomatoes and simmer for about 40 minutes until you have a thick sauce. Season to taste. Cut the peppers lengthways into even strips. Heat the remaining oil in a separate pan and sauté the peppers for a couple of minutes. Add the red wine and cook until it is reduced by half, then add the tomato sauce and most of the basil leaves and continue to cook for about 30 minutes. Check the seasoning, and serve drizzled with olive oil and scattered with the rest of the basil leaves.

BRAISED LENTILS WITH SWISS CHARD, TURNIPS AND PARSLEY RAVIOLI

This is my favourite vegetarian dish, using the neglected Swiss chard with turnips and a clean, fresh parsley ravioli. The bouquet garni is essential to add flavouring. And if you happen to have any asparagus peelings, add these too — they give incredible flavour to stock. The whole thing comes together like a sauce at the end. If you don't want to have a go at making your own ravioli, the lentils and sauce are delicious on their own.

SERVES 4

150g Puy lentils, rinsed / 1 small bouquet garni / 10 baby turnips (or 2 medium turnips) / a bunch of Swiss chard (about 250g) / 1 medium carrot / 1 small leek / olive oil / sea salt and freshly ground black pepper / a bunch of flat-leaf parsley / 50ml olive oil / 80g Parmesan cheese, grated / 250g pasta dough (see page 165)/ 1 egg, beaten with 1 teaspoon water

SAUCE

olive oil / 2 small shallots, peeled and finely chopped / 100ml dry white wine / 500ml vegetable stock / 50ml double cream / 80g unsalted butter

Bring a large pan of salted water to the boil, add the lentils and bouquet garni, and cook for about 15 minutes. Blanch the baby turnips in boiling salted water for 2–3 minutes, then peel and quarter. If using larger turnips, blanch for 4–5 minutes and cut into eighths. Remove the leaves from the Swiss chard and shred, then cut the stalks into 1cm dice and blanch them in boiling salted water for 1–2 minutes. Finely dice the carrot and leek. Heat a little olive oil in a pan, add the carrot, leek and a little salt, and cook gently until soft. Add the turnips, chard leaves and stems, carrots and leeks to the lentils.

To make the sauce, heat a little olive oil in a small pan, add the shallots and a little salt, and cook gently until soft. Add the wine and continue to cook until there is only a little liquid left. Add the vegetable stock and cook until reduced by half, then add the cream and whisk in the butter. Season and put aside.

To make the ravioli, pick the parsley leaves. Reserve a few, and blanch and refresh the rest. Squeeze out any water from the parsley, then purée with the olive oil and Parmesan. Shape into eight balls of approximately 15–20g each, and put in the fridge to firm up. Roll out the pasta till it's very thin, then cut out sixteen discs about 5cm across and wrap each one in clingfilm until ready to use. Take half the discs and brush the outside of each one with the egg. Place a cheese ball in the centre of each one, then take the remaining discs and place on top. Seal the edges, removing any air from the ravioli. Trim each ravioli to a round shape, using a pair of scissors. Cook in boiling water with a little olive oil and salt for 30 seconds and refresh in iced water.

To serve, combine the lentils and vegetables with the sauce and stir in the reserved chopped parsley. Reheat the ravioli in boiling water for 2½ minutes and serve with the lentils.

Chefs should stop worrying about what other chefs think and cook for the customers – not for themselves or to impress their colleagues. In all my restaurants there's a chef's table that customers can book so they can eat in the kitchen. In most kitchens the chefs never come into contact with their customers, and that's dangerous because it's easy for them to lose touch with what's going on in the restaurant.

The chef's table is great fun for the guests and a fantastic way of putting the chefs on the spot. There's no set format and no menu. The chefs spontaneously cook whatever's available fresh that morning – line-caught baby turbot, hand-picked courgette flowers or a beautiful piece of middle white pork. It keeps the chefs on their toes, draws out the creativity inside them and puts them to the test. It helps them improve their social skills in dealing with customers at an early stage and to gain in confidence. If they're going to be a great head chef, they have to be the best communicators in the business.

It's fascinating to see how the cooks create the dishes. You can give six different chefs exactly the same set of ingredients and each one of them will come up with their individual interpretation.

When I was interviewing new head chefs for the Walnut Tree, I used this test to quickly identify their strengths and creativity in the kitchen. You can see straight away the ones that are naturally turned on by food and the ones that are just looking for a weekly wage. One of the interviewees, an Italian chef who'd worked in kitchens around the world, not only confessed to using a microwave but kept control of a chaotic kitchen by meditating half-way through service – surely the 'ping' must have woken him up? His pasta dish was so overcooked that when I stuck my fork in the middle it came off the plate in one large lump. Surprisingly enough, putting him on the spot made us realize he wasn't the man for the job.

soups

'Soups are wonderfully versatile — they can make a meal in them-selves for lunch or the most amazing starter for dinner'

When I think of soup, I can't help but think of my childhood because of the sort of homely soups that my mum used to make, such as big steaming bowls of minestrone. With some second and third helpings, and with some crusty bread, it became a main meal for us.

I first had the pumpkin and Parmesan soup in the South of France, and it was my first experience of a silky, velvety soup. I'd gone to Cannes to work in a ski resort, and brought the idea back with me to London. We use lots of pumpkin soup in my restaurants now. Soup is often thought of as chunky, or rustic, but it can also be quite dainty and sophisticated — for example, the smoked haddock soup with poached quail's eggs. Again, a meal on its own.

But my all-time favourite, I have to be honest, is the most amazing French onion soup — gratinated, bubbling away, bursting with onions, croûtons, Gruyère cheese . . . and I always like to finish it with a touch of mustard as well.

When making soup the stock should be boiling, so that the cooking time is as short as possible and the soup doesn't end up stewed and stale. If you cook a soup quickly, it retains its freshness.

MINESTRONE

This is a classic Italian soup, full of many different textures and vegetables. But it's also a little bit more than a soup – it's almost a main course that you can eat with crusty bread for lunch. The idea behind most soups is to cook them as quickly as possible to keep all the freshness in. This dish is a prime example of needing to cook all the ingredients gently first in the oil and then adding the stock while it's boiling. This way you're not stewing it for hours and hours and losing all the goodness out of the vegetables. The thickener of this soup, although it's got tomato purée and all the vegetables in there, is the starch from the pasta, so don't panic if the soup is looking a bit thin at first.

SERVES 4
olive oil / 1 large red onion, peeled and chopped / 1 clove of garlic, peeled and crushed / 1 teaspoon fresh rosemary leaves, finely chopped / 250g pancetta or smoked streaky bacon, cut into lardons / 1 medium carrot, peeled and diced / 1 small swede, peeled and diced / 2 sticks of celery, trimmed and chopped / 1 medium leek, trimmed and chopped / sea salt and freshly ground black pepper / 1 tablespoon tomato purée / 2 litres chicken or vegetable stock / 100g spaghetti / ½ of a Savoy cabbage, roughly chopped / 250g mangetouts, halved / 15 cherry tomatoes, halved / pesto (see page 235)

Heat a little olive oil in a large pan and lightly sauté the onion, garlic and rosemary until softened. Add the pancetta or bacon and cook without colouring for 3–4 minutes until the fat begins to come out, then add the carrot, swede, celery and leek and cook for 2–3 minutes until they begin to soften. Season the vegetables while they're cooking in the pan. Add the tomato purée, stir, and continue cooking for 1 minute. Then add the hot stock. Turn down to a simmer and continue to cook for a further 15 minutes.

Put the spaghetti into a clean tea-towel and roll it up so you've got a sausage shape. Hold both ends tightly, then place it on a table and run it over the edge so that the spaghetti breaks up into small even pieces. Add to the soup and simmer until the spaghetti is tender – it should take about 10 minutes. Add the cabbage, mangetouts and tomatoes and cook for 5 minutes more. Check the seasoning, then serve the soup in bowls and top each with a spoonful of pesto. Eat with crusty bread. Perfect comfort food for a wintry day.

TURNIP, MARROW AND POTATO SOUP

This is quite an old-fashioned type of soup. It has a real homely flavour that reminds me of my childhood. Marrow is such an under-rated English vegetable and is used less and less in cooking these days. As a result, I don't think I can name any restaurants that have marrow on the menu, which is a shame.

It's a very quick soup to make, retaining all the goodness of the ingredients. For a bit of variety, freshen it up with some spinach. Just throw some washed leaves in at the end and let the residual heat cook it so the soup gains a nice, fresh green colour.

SERVES 4

1 large turnip, peeled / 1 medium marrow / 4–5 medium potatoes, peeled / 40g butter / sea salt and freshly ground black pepper / 500ml milk / 25g vermicelli / a handful of baby spinach, shredded / 3 tablespoons chopped fresh chervil

Cut the turnip, marrow and potatoes into 1cm dice. Heat the butter in a large pan, then add the vegetables and let them cook for a few minutes. Season well, then add the milk with 500ml of water and simmer for 5 minutes. When the vegetables are almost cooked, add the vermicelli and spinach. Cook for 15 minutes, until the vermicelli is tender. Add the chervil and serve.

FRENCH ONION SOUP

This is an authentic French soup. It's very simple to make – you just need to understand what to do with the onions when you caramelize them in the butter. Don't use anything other than butter for this, because it's a really great way of giving flavour to the onions. Don't be tempted to add any sugar – the natural sugars will come out of the onions as they cook. Just be sure to keep your eye on them, stirring them every now and again, and they will caramelize nice and evenly.

The idea behind topping the soup off with the baguette and Gruyère cheese is that when it all goes in the oven, the baguette absorbs the soup and becomes a nice crusty topping. A little twist to this recipe would be to add flakes of confit duck. Or you could finish it off with a dash of Worcestershire sauce. Or some mustard.

SERVES 4
75g butter / 400g onions, peeled and sliced / 2 bay leaves / 2 tablespoons sherry vinegar / 1 tablespoon flour / 1.5 litres brown chicken stock (see page 237) / 4 slices of baguette / 150g Gruyère cheese, grated

Heat the butter in a large pan and fry the onions and bay leaves slowly until golden brown and caramelized. Add the vinegar and stir to deglaze the pan, scraping up all the brown residue. Sprinkle in the flour and cook for a couple of minutes. Add the hot stock and bring to the boil, then turn the heat down and simmer for approximately 30 minutes. Preheat the oven to 240°C/475°F/gas 9. Serve the soup in heatproof bowls and top each with a slice of baguette and a sprinkling of Gruyère. Place the bowls on a baking tray in the preheated oven until the soup is bubbling up through the bread and the cheese is golden brown.

PUMPKIN AND PARMESAN SOUP

For this recipe you need to buy really good-quality pumpkins: nice and ripe. If you try to make this with pumpkins that aren't ripe, the end result will be tasteless and anaemic. You can check whether a pumpkin is ripe by the colour and texture of the skin. Usually, the darker brown the better quality it is, and it should be quite wrinkly too. When you take a section out of it with a spoon or a knife the inside should be a really bright orange colour, and it should smell strongly of sweet pumpkin. Be careful with seasoning this soup, as the Parmesan is naturally salty. It's best to season it at the end, once it's all cooked and puréed.

SERVES 4
40g butter / 2kg ripe pumpkin, peeled and chopped / 25g Parmesan cheese, grated / 1.2 litres good chicken stock / 3 tablespoons double cream / sea salt and freshly ground black pepper

Put the butter in a large pan over a medium heat, and when it has melted, add the pumpkin. Turn up the heat and cook quickly until the pumpkin is completely soft, then stir in the Parmesan and add the hot stock. Turn the heat down and simmer for a further 10 minutes. Leave to cool slightly, then blend in a food processor. Pass through a fine sieve back into the pan and stir in the cream. Bring back to the boil, season, and serve.

Cullen Skink. An old highland recipe

SMOKED HADDOCK SOUP WITH QUAIL'S EGGS

In my opinion, smoked haddock is the most under-rated, cheap, luxury ingredient that can be bought. It really should be up there alongside caviar, lobster and salmon. It has a lovely flavour and is relatively inexpensive.

For this soup, make sure you use undyed haddock so that the soup doesn't turn out a horrible bright yellow colour – so unappetizing. First you poach the haddock in milk infused with a bay leaf and maybe some thyme, leaving it just slightly undercooked. Then you're going to use this haddock-flavoured milk to make the soup; it will give it a lovely light smoked flavour. I suggest that you flake the haddock up to give the soup some texture. Retain a few flakes for garnishing.

With the lightly poached quail's eggs, when you cut into them the soft yolk will run into the soup adding another dimension to the dish.

SERVES 4
500ml milk / 1 bay leaf / 565g undyed smoked haddock, skinned / 1 onion, peeled and finely chopped / 1 large leek, trimmed and finely chopped / 1 potato, peeled and thinly sliced / 40g butter / sea salt and freshly ground white pepper / 12 quail's eggs, lightly poached (see page 236) / fresh flat-leaf parsley, to serve

Heat the milk in a large pan with the bay leaf and leave to infuse for 10 minutes. Add the haddock and poach gently for 3–4 minutes. Take the haddock out of the poaching liquid (reserving the liquid) and flake it. Set aside a little of the haddock for garnishing. In another large pan, cook the onion, leek and potato gently in the butter until the potato is softened. Add the haddock and the reserved liquid. Bring to the boil, then leave to cool slightly. Liquidize and pass through a sieve, then reheat if necessary. Season to taste with sea salt and white pepper. Divide into bowls and serve, each garnished with a few flakes of haddock, 3 warm, seasoned poached quail's eggs, and a sprinkling of chopped parsley.

BUTTER BEAN, BACON AND PARSLEY SOUP

This is a nice, rustic, peasant type of soup. Pulses are great to use in recipes as they are extremely cheap, and if you treat them correctly you'll get great results. Butter beans and lentils make fantastic soups as long as you impart plenty of flavour into them during the cooking process. I've done this here by cooking them with good-quality smoky bacon and bay leaves.

When you add the beans to the vegetables, it's important that you add the cooking liquor from the beans as well. A lot of people make the mistake of throwing any cooking water away, but it's so important to utilize it as that is where all the flavours are contained — whether you've used a bouquet garni, or a bay leaf, or bacon or peppercorns.

SERVES 4
225g dried butter beans, soaked overnight / 100g smoked streaky bacon, cut into lardons / 1 bay leaf / a sprig of thyme / sea salt and freshly ground black pepper / 25g butter / 2 tablespoons groundnut oil / 1 onion, peeled and finely chopped / 1 leek, trimmed and finely chopped / 2 sticks of celery, finely chopped / 1 clove of garlic, chopped / 140ml milk / 3 tablespoons chopped fresh parsley / extra virgin olive oil

Drain the soaked beans. Rinse them well with fresh water, drain again, and place in a large pan. Cover with water, and add the bacon pieces, bay leaf, thyme and seasoning. Bring to the boil, then turn the heat down and simmer for 20–30 minutes until the beans are tender. During this time, take a spoon and skim any white frothy residue off the top.

In another pan, heat the butter and groundnut oil and cook the onion, leek, celery and garlic gently for about 10 minutes. Add the beans and their cooking liquid, cook for a further 10 minutes, then gently mash the beans to thicken the soup. Add the milk and season. Stir in the chopped parsley and drizzle some good olive oil over each serving.

ROASTED PEPPER GAZPACHO

With this recipe I wanted to bring another dimension to the classic tomato gazpacho soup. We're really giving it much more depth of flavour by sautéing off the peppers first, as this brings out the natural sweetness inside them. If you take a raw pepper and taste it on its own, it's quite watery, but once you've cooked it for a little while in olive oil, seasoned lightly with herbs, it has a much more intense flavour. Doing this first, before you make the soup, really gives this dish much more depth. This soup improves with age, so you can eat it over the next couple of days and it will only get better.

SERVES 4
3 large red peppers / 3 tablespoons olive oil / 4 shallots, chopped / a sprig of fresh thyme / 1 small bay leaf / 1 clove of garlic, crushed / 3 large sprigs of fresh basil, including stalks / 6 or 7 very ripe plum tomatoes, chopped, seeds remaining / 800ml good tomato juice / sea salt and freshly ground black pepper / 100ml double cream / a few drops of Tabasco sauce / 1 tablespoon tomato purée

Quarter, deseed and slice the peppers. Heat the oil in a large pan and sauté the shallots, thyme, bay leaf and garlic without colouring until soft. Add the peppers and basil and cook on a high heat for about 5 minutes, until the peppers soften. Then turn the heat down, cover the pan, and cook slowly for 10–15 minutes, stirring occasionally. This intensifies the flavour of the peppers – they will taste amazing. Take off the heat and add the tomatoes, tomato juice and seasoning. Leave to marinate overnight if you can. Remove all the herbs and blend the soup in a food processor until smooth. Add the cream, Tabasco and tomato purée and blend again briefly. Pass the soup through a fine sieve and adjust the seasoning. Chill well before serving.

You have to make mistakes in order to learn, but it's every chef's job to keep the mistakes in the kitchen. You're living in a fantasy land if you think you can be a successful chef without being reprimanded for your cock-ups. It's a bit like learning a foreign language: you have to be prepared to sound stupid at first and be criticised before you can speak it fluently.

When I was working at Harvey's with Marco Pierre White, one of his signature dishes was a beautiful terrine made with poached leeks and Dublin bay prawns. It looked like the most intricate mosaic and it tasted heavenly. In those days it cost £100 to make and Marco put it on the menu at £20 a slice. As I was the most senior chef, it was my job to put it together. On one occasion I had asked my commis chef to cook the prawns – to blanch them for thirty seconds, then peel while warm and poach for a further three to four minutes in court-bouillon. I assumed he'd cooked them to perfection.

I spent the entire night making the terrine. The next day when we came to slice it, I couldn't believe what I saw. There they were: four big raw prawns running through each slice. My commis chef had only blanched them for thirty seconds and had failed to poach them. Marco liked to get things off his chest straight away so I knew I was in trouble. He docked my wages and he didn't give up his verbal rant until he'd drummed it into my head what a complete and utter balls-up I'd made. It's the kind of mistake you only make once in your life, but it taught me that you can't work at the top of your profession unless you can take SAS-style grillings. The stronger the bollocking, the quicker you learn.

fish

'I adore cooking and eating fish, and love to buy my fish whole because that way I can see what I'm getting'

I was once very privileged to spend some time as a chef on a luxury yacht. It was my perfect dream working holiday, where I could earn a fortune and travel the world — from Sardinia, Sicily and Corsica to Antigua and the British Virgin Islands — and it meant that I could cook some of the freshest fish ever. Not only were my cooking skills kept up to the mark, but I'd become an advanced diver by the end of the trip. There were times when I was spending more time under water than in the galley, and I was getting paid for it!

When you're buying fish, a local fishmonger can be fantastic. The advantage is that he'll fillet it for you and you've then got the bones to make great stock (see page 233). There is absolutely nothing wrong with buying fish in a supermarket, though, as the majority of them now have great fish counters. Or, even better, go out and catch your own. In May my family take the chance to get away and do some trout fishing on the River Test near Romsey. On a good day I can pull out between eight and ten brown trout within twenty minutes, so I can be in and out without a permit because I'm so good! Growing up in Scotland, going back and forth to the lochs, catching my first salmon was a huge landmark in my life. I can't wait to take my son, Jack, when he's old enough.

SEA BREAM WITH ROASTED FENNEL, OLIVES, CLAMS, GARLIC AND THYME

This is a dish that I used to cook for the staff when I was working as head chef on the yacht. We were based out in the bay at Cannes one summer – the boat was seventy metres long and couldn't come into the pier, so a speedboat would take me to the market in the morning to go shopping. It was here that I came across these really nice fish called dorade – which are better known in Britain as bream.

One day at the end of September, I prepared and cooked a perfect pink dorade for every-one – all the ingredients were fresh and fragrant and oozed of the Med. When the owners weren't entertaining on the boat we could do a lot more for the staff and we had an absolute ball – I would treat them like restaurant customers and they loved it. They would be used to spaghetti bolognese and cottage pie, so these dishes were in a different dimension.

SERVES 4
1kg fresh clams / 1 shallot, sliced / 300ml white wine / 8 baby fennel / olive oil / sea salt and freshly ground black pepper / 24 black olives, stoned / 24 cherry tomatoes, halved / 2 cloves of garlic, crushed / a bunch of fresh thyme, leaves picked / optional: 2 sprigs of fresh tarragon, leaves picked / 250ml lemon and basil infused olive oil (see page 221) / 4 x 400g bream, filleted and pinboned

Clean the clams thoroughly and discard any open ones. Place them in a large pan with the sliced shallot and wine, cover and bring to the boil. Turn the heat down and simmer with the lid on for 5 minutes, then drain. Pick the clam meat from the shells and place in a bowl, covered with clingfilm.

Meanwhile, preheat the oven to 180°C/350°F/gas 4. Place the fennel on a baking tray and lightly drizzle olive oil over them, then season and cook in the preheated oven until soft and golden. Put the clams, olives, tomatoes, garlic, thyme and tarragon leaves (if using) into a large pan over a medium heat, then season and pour in the lemon-infused oil. Bring up to a simmer and remove from the heat. Put to one side and leave the flavours to infuse for 30 minutes.

Score the fillets of bream on the skin side and season. Heat a few tablespoons of olive oil in a frying pan and cook the bream, skin side down, for about 3 minutes. Turn the fish over and cook for a further 2 minutes. Spoon the clam mixture on to four warm plates and top with two fillets of bream each. Divide the roast fennel between the plates and serve.

POACHED SEA TROUT WITH ASPARAGUS
AND MINT HOLLANDAISE

This dish doesn't really need potatoes, but if they're in season then lovely Jersey Royals can be boiled in their skins for maximum flavour and then skinned when they have cooled down. Instead of sea trout you could use salmon, red mullet or rainbow trout. This is one of the healthiest dishes to eat because you've got the natural flavour from the court-bouillon. And it can be served warm rather than hot, which is always a help when you're cooking for a bunch of people. I just love the integrity and simplicity of this. The flavours are vibrant, the asparagus is healthy, and the summery, fresh mint hollandaise just tops it all off.

SERVES 4
4 x 150g fillets of sea trout, skinned and boned / salt and freshly ground black pepper / 2 bunches of green asparagus / 2 bunches of white asparagus / a small knob of butter / classic vinaigrette (see page 217) / a bunch of fresh chives, finely chopped / mint hollandaise (see page 229)

POACHING LIQUOR
1.5 litres fish stock (see page 233) or water / a sprig of fresh thyme / a few fresh basil stalks / 2–3 slices of lemon / 2 sticks of lemon grass, roughly chopped / a pinch of sea salt

Put the ingredients for the poaching liquor into a large pan, bring to the boil, then simmer for 15–20 minutes so the flavours infuse. Add the seasoned sea trout fillets and let these poach gently for 4–5 minutes, then remove the pan from the heat and leave the fish to cool in the liquid for a couple of minutes.

Peel, trim and blanch the asparagus spears for 2–3 minutes until tender but still slightly firm, mix them with some melted butter and season. If using potatoes, crush them with the back of a fork so they break into uneven chunks. Season well and drizzle with a little vinaigrette. Add the chives and mix well. Place some potato on each warm plate, place the fish on top, and serve with the asparagus and a spoonful of the mint hollandaise.

CLASSIC DOVER SOLE WITH MASHED POTATO AND FRENCH PEAS

The Dover sole is the Rolls-Royce of the fish world – it's a British classic and we should be incredibly proud of it. In London's five-star hotels (from the Connaught, to the Savoy, to Claridge's) it has been ordered as a comfort food by customers for years. As it hasn't become a trendy fish we haven't started farming it, like sea bass, halibut, cod and salmon – they have become so hip that they are now farmed and the quality isn't as good as when line-caught.

Dover sole has a stand-alone flavour that doesn't need to be breadcrumbed, stuffed with lobster mousse, or cut into goujons. All it needs is to be pan-fried or grilled. Don't tart it up. Lemon sole is another favourite – it's a little less powerful than a Dover sole. My wife, Tana, has always cooked it for our kids – it's a good way of introducing sole to them as it's slightly easier on the palate. It's also a striking white colour, with yellow spots on its skin – the kids love to look out for them at the fishmonger's.

SERVES 4
1kg large La Ratte potatoes / sea salt and freshly ground black pepper / 100ml milk / 250g butter / 2 shallots, finely sliced / 500g peas (frozen petits pois are good) / 140ml chicken stock / 2 baby gem lettuces, finely shredded / 4 x 500g Dover sole on the bone, skinned, heads removed and trimmed / flour, for dusting / olive oil for frying / 2½ lemons

First put the potatoes into a large pan, cover with cold water and season well. Bring to the boil, then lower the heat and simmer for 15–20 minutes, until tender. Drain the potatoes in a colander and peel them while they're still hot. To mash them use a potato masher, or try pushing them through a fine sieve, which will give you really smooth mash. Meanwhile, heat the milk. Beat 100g of the butter into the mashed potato and season. As the milk boils, add it to the potatoes. Keep warm until ready to serve.

Sauté the sliced shallots in about 50g of the butter until soft, add the peas and cook for a couple of minutes. Pour on the chicken stock and simmer for about 10 minutes, until the peas are cooked and the stock has reduced by half. Stir in the shredded lettuce and cook for a further 2 minutes.

Season the sole and lightly dust with flour. Heat up a little oil and 50g of the butter in a large pan. Fry the fish for about 6 minutes on each side until golden and the flesh comes away from the bone. Place each sole on a large plate with a dollop of mashed potato on one side and a spoonful of peas on the other. Put the pan back on the heat, add the remaining butter and swirl it about until it foams and turns a nut-brown colour. Add a squeeze of lemon and then spoon the butter over the fish. Serve with half a lemon on each plate.

FILLET OF HALIBUT ON A BED OF SPINACH WITH MUSCAT GRAPES AND FISH CREAM

Fish and fruit can sometimes be a good combination – for instance, halibut or turbot cooked with pink grapefruit juice is amazing. You may be surprised that I'm using grapes here, but they work really well. Little sexy seedless ones, such as Muscat, are great. It's like the marriage of fish with wine – like having a lovely chilled glass of Muscat or Chablis.

An absolute classic at catering college is sole with white grapes, and this is an updated version where we're not glazing it or making a sauce to go with it, just a lovely light fish cream made with Noilly Prat vermouth. It gives a nice balance to a fish that's been roasted in a pan and then braised in its juices. The cream adds a subtleness to the dish. I've also used baby spinach to go with the fish as it is so delicate and dainty.

SERVES 4

4 x 150g halibut fillets, skinned / olive oil / 50ml fish stock (see page 233) / 50g butter / 400g baby leaf spinach / 350g Muscat (or white) grapes, peeled / ½ a bunch of chervil, finely chopped

FISH CREAM

15g butter / 4 shallots, peeled and finely chopped / 250ml dry white wine / 250ml Noilly Prat vermouth / 500ml fish stock (see page 233) / 500ml double cream / sea salt and freshly ground black pepper

Preheat the oven to 180°C/350°F/gas 4. To make the fish cream, heat the butter in a wide saucepan and gently sweat the shallots until soft. Add the wine and vermouth and simmer until the liquid has reduced by half. Pour in the stock and reduce by half again. Stir in the cream and continue to reduce until the sauce has the consistency of pouring cream. Season and strain through a fine sieve.

In an ovenproof non-stick pan, fry the halibut fillets in olive oil on one side until golden brown. Turn them over and continue to cook for 1 minute. Add the fish stock. Transfer to the oven for 4–5 minutes, basting occasionally to keep the fish moist. Meanwhile, melt the 50g of butter in a pan and toss the spinach in it until it wilts lightly. Add the grapes to the fish cream and warm through. Divide the spinach between four warm plates and place the halibut fillets on top. Spoon the grapes and fish cream around the edge and sprinkle over the chervil.

GRILLED LOBSTER AND CHIPS

As with the lobster roll on page 46, I first came across this recipe at the Gramercy Tavern in New York and I've since put it on the menu at the Boxwood Café. The best lobsters to use are Scottish or Canadian, or the Dorset Blue, which are cultivated in shallow warm waters so their shells are softer. The prime lobster has to be the Scottish, though — with its very subtle flavour, it's like gold dust.

We all enjoy fish and chips and I love the idea of eating lobster and chips. There is no reason to be embarrassed about eating chips. And with a whole roasted lobster in its shell you can't go wrong. You'll get a great flavour and you'll be able to dip your chips in the head to mop up all the lovely juices! You can finish the lobster off by brushing it with garlic butter, or rosemary or basil butter.

SERVES 4
4 x 500g lobsters / 4–5 large Maris Piper potatoes / vegetable oil / 75g butter / 2 cloves of garlic, crushed / 30g flat-leaf parsley, chopped / sea salt and freshly ground black pepper

To kill your lobsters, see page 240. Plunge them into a large pan of boiling salted water, then reduce the heat to a simmer and cook for 2 minutes. Remove them from the pan and leave to cool slightly. With a large knife, cut the lobsters in half lengthways and crack the claws. Cut the potatoes into fine frites, and blanch them in vegetable oil at 140°C/275°F until softened. Drain them on kitchen paper. Turn the heat up to 180°C/350°F and fry until crisp and golden. Meanwhile, melt the butter in a large frying pan and add the garlic. Cook for a couple of minutes, then add the chopped parsley. Quickly toss in the chips and season.

While the chips are cooking, heat a grill or griddle. Lay the lobsters on it, flesh side down, and cook for 4–6 minutes. Serve with the chips and a lightly dressed and seasoned rocket and shaved Parmesan salad.

ROAST SKATE WITH BEETROOT AND PARMESAN

Skate and brown butter (beurre noisette) is a combination that all chefs become familiar with when they start cooking. I would never poach a skate, as it doesn't hold the flavour, and adding beetroot sweetens up the robust roasting process. This is a nice way to give a different texture and lightness and confirms it as a healthy dish. Skate is a fish that has become a delicacy now – no one would have thought so ten years ago. It has to be used within twenty-four hours of purchasing, though, because as it starts to relax it releases ammonia – a very pungent smell, so you have to get it cooked quickly and not let it sit about for too long!

Parmesan is lovely with skate – either shaved over at the end, or diced using a softer variety such as Gran Padana. The natural salt from the cheese seasons the whole dish. Serve the fish just as the cheese starts to melt.

SERVES 4
2 large beetroots / rock salt / 4 medium skate wings / salt and freshly ground pepper / olive oil / 100g butter / 3 tablespoons small capers / 100g Parmesan cheese / 4 tablespoons chopped flat-leaf parsley / ½ a lemon / classic vinaigrette (see page 217)

Preheat the oven to 180°C/350°F/gas 4. Wrap the beetroots in foil, lay them on a bed of rock salt, and bake them for 2 hours, until soft. Cool, peel and dice into 1cm cubes. Season the skate wings well. Heat the oil in a pan until hot. Brown the skate on one side for 2–3 minutes. Turn over and add the butter. When it foams and turns golden, baste the fish and cook for 3–4 minutes, then add the capers and beetroot to the pan and cook for a further 2 minutes, continually spooning the butter over the fish. Remove the pan from the heat, and add the Parmesan, parsley and a squeeze of lemon. Glaze with the vinaigrette.

FISH PIE

The nice thing about this pie is that it can ease the pressure of a busy day – it can be made in the morning and then baked when you're ready to sit down. Remember to cut your fish into even-sized small pieces so they cook in the same time. Try using salmon, cod or prawns – if you're feeling wealthy you could buy the big tiger prawns. Pieces of halibut are also good, or brill. It's best to go and have a look in the fishmonger's to see what they've got – and ask for any trimmings they might have.

The Glass House had Thai fishcakes with chilli dressing on their menu but I thought it would be a good idea instead to use local fish from the lake to go in a fish pie, as it was closer to what the Glass House was about. I decided to use Windermere char as the basis of the pie. In order to make any decent money in a restaurant, with no waste, it is important to utilize local ingredients, especially if they cost nothing, they're already in place and you can use every single bit. They now have Glass House fish pie on the menu and I really believe that it could do for them what shepherd's pie has done for the Ivy in London.

SERVES 4
1 x fish cream (see page 121) / 800g fish (see above) / sea salt and freshly ground black pepper / ½ a lemon / a couple of sprigs of fresh tarragon, leaves picked and chopped / 1 tablespoon chopped fresh flat-leaf parsley / 5 large Désirée potatoes / a little milk and butter / 2 large egg yolks

Preheat the oven to 180°C/350°F/gas 4. Make the fish cream. Cut your fish into bite-sized pieces. Season them and mix with the fish cream. Add a little squeeze of lemon juice, the chopped tarragon and parsley, and bind together well. Pour into an earthenware dish. Because the fish is raw all the juices stay in the dish, meaning you don't lose any flavour at all.

Cook the potatoes in boiling salted water until tender, and mash with a little milk and butter until smooth. Stir in the raw egg yolks, then either pipe the mash over the fish or spoon it so it's nice and rustic-looking. Cook the fish pie in the preheated oven for approximately 20 minutes until bubbling and golden brown. Serve with some buttered petit pois or spinach.

JERUSALEM ARTICHOKE RISOTTO WITH SCALLOPS

This is a really good way to use Jerusalem artichokes without all the fuss of having to peel them first. Many restaurants peel them and then put them into acidulated water to stop them going brown, but this just results in lemon-flavoured artichokes and a horrible, sour purée when they're cooked. It's no good having a beautiful white colour to the purée but no taste. With this recipe the purée will be slightly off-white but it will have a lovely intense flavour. When you stir it into the risotto it adds a real earthiness. I offset the richness of the risotto and sautéd scallops with a drizzle of sweet sherry caramel.

SERVES 2
olive oil / 200g risotto rice / 500ml chicken stock / 200g Jerusalem artichokes, washed and sliced / 100g butter / 100ml cream / 25g Parmesan cheese, grated / sea salt and freshly ground black pepper / 8 large scallops, sliced / 50g sugar / 50ml sherry vinegar

Heat a few tablespoons of olive oil in a pan, add the rice and stir for 2–3 minutes so the rice absorbs the oil. Add the hot stock a little at a time, stirring constantly, until it has all been absorbed and the rice is cooked. This should take around 25–30 minutes. Meanwhile, cook the artichokes in 50g of the butter until soft. Add the cream. Reduce down until the cream has almost evaporated and the artichokes are velvety in texture, stirring every now and then to make sure it's not catching on the bottom of the pan. Purée in a food processor.

Mix the artichoke purée into the rice and add the remaining 50g of butter and the Parmesan. Check for seasoning. Slice each scallop into 3 pieces and sauté in hot oil for 1 minute on each side until they're medium rare. Place on top of the risotto. In a heavy-based pan, heat the sugar until it's a dark golden colour. Carefully add the sherry vinegar and reduce until you have a thick syrup. Drizzle this over the risotto and serve.

FILLETS OF COD WITH CHORIZO

This is a stunning dish which you can make with any meaty fish, and it's especially good with cod or monkfish. You need some nice thick cod fillets and from there you just throw everything in together: the tomatoes, the basil and the chorizo. The dish makes its own sauce with the juice from the cod, the sherry and the tomatoes. It's quite a spicy dish because the paprika from the chorizo mixes in with the sauce. When you remove the foil the most wonderful aroma hits you — just delicious. Good with buttered cabbage.

SERVES 4
4 tablespoons olive oil / 4 x 175g cod fillets / 8 cherry tomatoes, quartered / 125g chorizo sausage, sliced / 4 tablespoons dry sherry / 8 large fresh basil leaves / sea salt and freshly ground black pepper / 1 lemon

Preheat the oven to 180°C/350°F/gas 4. Drizzle some oil into four heatproof dishes and place a cod fillet in each one. Divide the tomatoes, chorizo, sherry and remaining olive oil between the dishes. Lay a couple of basil leaves on the top and season well. Cover each dish tightly with foil and bake in the preheated oven for 10–20 minutes, depending upon the thickness of the fish, until it is cooked. Remove the foil and squeeze a little lemon juice over.

DAUBE OF SQUID

This is a rustic, Provençal type of dish and is a different take on the classic daube, which is usually done with beef. This method lends itself really well to squid, which is quite firm and meaty in texture but becomes nice and tender. Marinating it first also helps to tenderize it. The marinade is lovely, made with lots and lots of lemon juice, which gives it a real sharpness that cuts through the richness of the other ingredients and lightens the dish up.

SERVES 4

1.5kg squid, cleaned and cut into 2.5cm pieces / 200ml white wine / 2 small lemons, sliced / 2 bay leaves / 2 cloves of garlic, chopped / 2 tablespoons chopped fresh flat-leaf parsley / sea salt and freshly ground black pepper / 3 tablespoons olive oil / 1 red onion, finely chopped / 500g plum tomatoes / 450g small new potatoes, halved

Place the squid, wine, lemon slices, bay leaves, garlic and parsley in a bowl. Season well, then leave to marinate for a couple of hours.

Heat the olive oil and fry the onion until soft. Keeping the marinade, drain the squid and add to the onion. Cook for 2 minutes, then add the tomatoes and cook for 5 minutes more. Discard the lemons and add the marinade to the squid. Cover and cook gently for about 2 hours, then add the potatoes and cook for a further 30 minutes. Season and serve.

CLASSIC BOUILLABAISSE

This is the classic Mediterranean fish soup, or stew. To make it properly you need to have a wide variety of fish, including rascasse, some fish with firm flesh, some small ones to disintegrate into the broth and maybe some shellfish as well. Ask your fishmonger for a good selection, and ask him to clean and scale it all for you if you don't fancy doing it yourself!

SERVES 4

2kg mixed fish (e.g. gurnard, John Dory, rascasse, whiting) / 1 clove of garlic, crushed / 150ml olive oil / 2 large onions, finely chopped / 2 large tomatoes, peeled, deseeded and chopped / 1 leek (the white bit only), finely chopped / a sprig of fresh thyme / 1 bay leaf / a pinch of saffron / 2 litres fish stock (see page 233) / sea salt and freshly ground black pepper / garlic mayonnaise (see page 228) / croûtons

Chop the fish into even-sized pieces, removing the heads if necessary. Place the fish, garlic, oil, onions, tomatoes, leek, thyme, bay leaf and saffron in a large pan and stir well. Heat the stock and pour over the fish to cover. Simmer for approximately 8–10 minutes until the fish is cooked, then check the seasoning. Serve with garlic mayonnaise and croûtons.

As a young cook in a kitchen, the worst thing you can say to your head chef is 'I'm tired.' I know if one of my team said that to me I'd be down on them like a ton of bricks. It suggests they're not firing on all cylinders or they've had a heavy session the night before. If they're not on their toes during service, then they're unlikely to produce their best work.

Spending time with the kitchen team at the Glass House was a rewarding experience. Some days I spent eighteen hours with them, perfecting the food, getting them excited about new dishes and teaching the young cooks new techniques. I still get a real buzz watching young talent progress. What I hadn't bargained for was that Randal, the kitchen porter, had been so fired up by the changes in the kitchen that he'd taken on new responsibilities of his own, such as operating the lift that delivered the food to the restaurant and making sure each plate of food he put in it was perfect. On my last day I caught him yawning at the sink. I asked if he was bored.

He replied, 'No, not bored, just haven't slept all week.'

I was anxious to know why and completely astonished by his answer: 'I've just got so much inspiration from watching you all work together, and for the first time in this job I've felt like part of the team.' I was chuffed to know that Randal had at last found some job satisfaction, but I encouraged him to go home and get some sleep . . . only not too much.

I told Randal about my experience in Paris when I was training with Guy Savoy. I arrived one Friday morning feeling exhausted at the end of a busy week. I made the mistake of telling him so.

'What do you mean, tired?' he said. 'How many hours did you sleep?'

I told him just six.

'Six? That's far too many. By the time you get to sixty you'll have slept for fifteen years. Does that scare you?'

'Yes,' I replied.

'Well, then, shut the fuck up, sleep for four hours and by the time you reach sixty you'll only have slept for ten!'

Randal made his way home, and slept for exactly four hours.

meat

'When it comes to cooking meat, I find it incredibly frustrating that some chefs ignore the cheaper cuts and instead go straight for the top-class fillets'

It's very easy for chefs to cook high-class cuts of meat and lazy of them to forget about every other cut. I think it's always testament to a young chef's skill if they can make something special out of something cheap. Ten years ago, when I opened Aubergine, if I couldn't use fillet I would use oxtail. Along with other cheap things like mashed potato and lentils, some of these dishes are still on the lunch menu today.

I want to tell you about a great test you can do, when you're cooking duck or beef for instance, using 'fingertip control'. This is about being able to identify how your meat is cooked simply by touching it. It's an important thing to know for any chef or enthusiast at home – simply touch the meat then go back 5 minutes later and touch it again. The amount of 'give' will tell you how well done it is. In the restaurants we are constantly touching, pushing and prodding with our fingers. If, for instance, you're cooking a fillet of beef, the hardest way in the world to cook it is blue. Of the chefs I know, 99 per cent of them will overcook it. All you need to do is take your meat out of the fridge, wait for it to come up to room temperature, then sear it for 10 seconds on each side. It will be lukewarm in the centre without being cooked. To get a steak 'blue to rare' your finger will almost go through the meat when you use fingertip control. Medium rare gives you pink meat but with the texture still nice and soft, and for 'medium rare to medium' there is little give in the steak and it becomes hugely reduced in size because all the blood has been taken out of it. As for 'well done' – there is nothing worse. I hate to see young chefs overcook meat.

However, as I explained to the staff up in Ambleside, if a customer wants something well done it's their prerogative as they are paying. I advised the chefs that when asked for 'well done' meat they should cook the meat medium with a ladle of stock added to the pan. During cooking the stock evaporates, glazes the meat and adds moisture so it doesn't end up dry and black. You don't have to add

STUFFED LOIN OF ROAST SUCKLING PIG
WITH CRISPY CRACKLING

This is a fantastic dish, especially for Sunday lunch with your family. Rather than worrying about how to bone the loin, ask your butcher to do it for you. It won't take him long and it means that all you have to do when you get home is flavour the meat and cook it. The great thing about this is there's no waste. The day after you've cooked it you can make the most amazing suckling pig sarnie (see page 47). The sage flavours the meat so well, but other herbs that also work are rosemary, bay leaves, tarragon, wild thyme and lemon thyme. And the salt helps to keep the crackling crisp.

SERVES 4
1kg short loin of suckling pig / 1 clove of garlic, peeled and crushed / sea salt and freshly ground black pepper / zest of 1 lemon / a bunch of fresh sage, leaves picked / a bunch of fresh flat-leaf parsley, leaves picked / olive oil

Preheat the oven to 220°C/425°F/gas 7. Lay the loin of pork skin side down on a work surface and lightly score it with a knife. Rub the garlic firmly over the meat to really get the flavour in there, then season it well and sprinkle with the lemon zest. Scatter the herbs over the middle of the pork loin, then roll it up tightly and secure it with some string, tied in a butcher's knot if you know how to do one of those. If not, just tie it tightly to make sure it won't come apart.

Oil the skin of the rolled pork and roast it in the preheated oven for 20–25 minutes. When cooked, it should be slightly pink in the middle and crisp and golden on the outside. If the crackling is soft and you want to crisp it up, just heat some olive oil in a pan and roll the pork in it until it spits and blisters. Serve with some fluffy mashed potato and broccoli.

BRAISED SHANK OF LAMB WITH PARSNIP PURÉE

I love this particular cut, as it's the part that people tend to forget. When I was little I grew up eating either leg of lamb or shank. The shank is a cheap, very earthy cut of meat and easy to cook, as you can start it off and then forget about it for a few hours. It benefits from a slow cooking process – the longer you cook it the better. During the process you can actually watch the meat slide down the shank, and the bone is great for presentation. If you're not a confident cook, this is a good cut to start with. Why serve it with parsnips? Well, I'm fed up with potatoes always being served with lamb. The sweetness of the purée really cuts through the richness of the meat. Parsnip goes hand in glove with lamb – two of the cheapest ingredients and they sit beautifully together.

SERVES 4
olive oil / sea salt and freshly ground black pepper / 4 small lamb shanks / 1 carrot, roughly chopped / 1 onion, roughly chopped / 1 leek, roughly chopped / 1 celery stick, roughly chopped / ½ a head of garlic / a sprig of fresh thyme / 1 bay leaf / a sprig of fresh rosemary / 2 star anise / 300ml dry white wine / 1 litre brown chicken stock (see page 237)

PARSNIP PURÉE
100g butter / 4 large parsnips, peeled and chopped / 100ml double cream / sea salt and freshly ground black pepper

Heat a little olive oil in a large pan. Season the lamb shanks and brown them all over in the oil, then remove from the pan and set aside. Add a little more oil to the pan, add the chopped vegetables, garlic, herbs and anise, and cook gently until browned. Pour in the wine and continue cooking until it has reduced down to a syrup. Put the shanks back into the pan and pour on the stock. Season to taste.

Cover the pan and cook gently for 2½–3 hours until the meat is tender and falls off the bone. About 30 minutes before the end of the cooking time, make the parsnip purée. Melt the butter in a frying pan over a low heat and cook the parsnips until completely soft and falling apart (about 25 minutes). Add the cream and bring to the boil. Season, then liquidize to a smooth purée. Keep warm.

Remove the lamb shanks from their liquid and keep warm. Strain the stock, pour it back into the pan and cook over a high heat until it forms a sauce consistency. Serve each shank with a good spoonful of the parsnip purée, and pour over the sauce. Lovely with some simple steamed broccoli or green beans.

POACHED CHICKEN LEGS WITH HERB DUMPLINGS AND TURNIPS

In all the restaurants that we have been working on, chicken legs are served to the staff, so I've tried to show the head chefs in these kitchens that even though they are a cheap cut they can also be used to make a beautiful meal like this. It's a rustic, peasant-style dish that's completely self-contained – a great one-pot wonder, especially if you're taking on board a table of ramblers who are going to be walking for the next few hours! The main secret is to keep the stock nice and clear, so while you're simmering the casserole, you need to remove the scum off the top using a teaspoon. The stock will turn into a flavoursome broth. Dumplings are something we seem to have forgotten about in this country, and they are just lovely with lots of flat-leaf parsley.

SERVES 4
sea salt and freshly ground black pepper / 4 large chicken legs / 3 large carrots, peeled / 2 medium onions, peeled / 2 sticks of celery, peeled / 3 large turnips, peeled / 2 cloves of garlic, peeled / a sprig of fresh thyme / 2–3 sprigs of fresh parsley / 1 star anise / 1 bay leaf / 1 litre good chicken stock or water

HERB DUMPLINGS
225g self-raising flour / 115g suet / 1 tablespoon chopped fresh flat-leaf parsley

Season the chicken legs and place them in a large pan. Chop the vegetables into large pieces and add to the chicken. Cut the garlic cloves in half and add to the pan along with the thyme, parsley sprigs, star anise and the bay leaf. Add enough chicken stock or water to just cover the chicken and vegetables. Put the pan on a medium heat and simmer gently, uncovered, for about 1 hour, skimming the liquid when necessary to achieve a good clear broth.

While the chicken is cooking, make the dumplings by mixing together the flour and suet with a pinch of salt, the chopped parsley and enough cold water to make the mixture into a soft dough. Roll into small balls. Towards the end of the cooking time, remove some of the poaching stock to a second pan and bring to a simmer. Drop the dumplings into the stock and poach for 10–15 minutes until soft and puffed up. Serve with the chicken and vegetables.

BRAISED OXTAIL IN BEEF TOMATOES

This is a really rich, intensely flavoured dish that reminds me of my early days spent working in Parisian cafés. It's quite a French main course – in the way it uses inexpensive ingredients and gets the most taste out of them. If you can, try to marinate the oxtail the day before you want to cook it, as this will really help the flavours to develop. It's a lovely way of eating oxtail and tomatoes together. You have to use beef tomatoes in this dish because they're more robust and substantial and can take the oven cooking, unlike vine tomatoes. If you don't want to serve the oxtail in tomatoes you could always try putting it into lasagne, stirring it into penne or spaghetti, or putting it into an earthenware dish with some mash on top to make a posh cottage pie. Any leftover trimmings are great to freeze for the next time you want to make oxtail and tomato soup.

SERVES 4

1 x 1.5kg whole oxtail, chopped / ½ a bottle of red wine / a sprig of fresh thyme / 1 bay leaf / olive oil / 2 carrots, peeled and coarsely chopped / 1 onion, peeled and coarsely chopped / 1 litre brown chicken stock (see page 237) / sea salt and freshly ground black pepper / 2 small handfuls of mixed herbs (parsley, tarragon, chives) / 4 large beef tomatoes, blanched and skinned

Put the oxtail pieces in a bowl with the wine, thyme and bay leaf and leave to marinate for at least 5–6 hours but overnight if possible.

When ready to use, preheat the oven to 180°C/350°F/gas 4. Remove the oxtail pieces from the bowl and pat dry with a clean cloth, reserving the marinade. Heat about 3 tablespoons of olive oil in a pan until smoking hot and carefully brown the oxtail pieces all over until almost black. Remove them from the pan and put them into an ovenproof dish.

Wipe the pan clean. Add 2 tablespoons of olive oil and cook the carrots and onion gently till soft. Add the reserved marinade and the stock and boil until reduced by half. Pour over the oxtail pieces, then transfer the dish to the oven and cook for 2½–3 hours, until the meat falls from the bone. Take the dish out of the oven, leaving the heat on. Remove the oxtail pieces from the dish and strain the stock through a fine sieve. Put the stock back on the heat and boil to reduce it to about 300ml. When the meat is cool enough to handle, pull it into smaller chunks, removing any fat, gristle or bone. Mix the meat with the reduced stock and season to taste. Mix in the chopped herbs and set aside.

Meanwhile, scoop out the insides of the tomatoes and season. Fill them with the oxtail mix, then put back in the oven for a few minutes to heat through.

SIRLOIN OF BEEF WITH ROASTED CHARLOTTE POTATOES AND RED WINE SHALLOTS

Charlotte potatoes are in the premier division of potatoes – they are waxy, with a dark yellow colour, incredibly flavoursome and the best potato to roast. At the Boxwood Café we use ribeye of beef for this recipe, but at home I suggest you use sirloin, or an individual ribeye. Even the T-bone steak, the retro classic, can be used as an alternative to sirloin. Don't be scared to serve this warm – there is nothing worse than being pressured into thinking you've got to serve it hot. I personally enjoy beef much better when it's warm, as it's been able to rest sufficiently, which tenderizes it.

SERVES 4
sea salt and freshly ground black pepper / 1 x 1kg sirloin beef / olive oil / 1 head of garlic, broken into cloves / a few sprigs of fresh thyme and a few thyme leaves / 12 large Charlotte potatoes, peeled / 150g unsalted butter / 16 medium shallots, peeled / 285ml port / 285ml red wine

Preheat the oven to 180°C/350°F/gas 4. Season the sirloin well, then heat some olive oil in a frying pan and brown the meat all over. Transfer it to an ovenproof dish. Add the garlic cloves, a sprig or two of thyme and a little fresh olive oil. Cook in the preheated oven for about 25 minutes, then remove the dish from the oven and set aside. With this timing the sirloin will be nice and rare – cook it for longer if you prefer.

Meanwhile, in another pan heat some more olive oil and colour the potatoes all over until nice and golden. Add a few more sprigs of thyme and the butter and cook slowly until they are soft in the middle – 15-20 minutes.

In a small pan, sauté the shallots in olive oil until slightly coloured. Drain off the excess oil and add the port, red wine and thyme leaves. Simmer until the liquid has reduced and the shallots are cooked and glazed like rubies. Cut the beef into generous slices and arrange in a serving dish with the potatoes, shallots and garlic.

BURGER AND CHIPS

Every chef in the country would be a hypocrite if they said they never ate burger and chips. The Boxwood Café burger has been the most amazing addition to the menu – we make it with veal and add some minced foie gras. We give it real three-star treatment, with beautiful chopped mushrooms on the bun and the most amazing onion relish. Here's a slightly different version but made along similar lines. The thing to remember is to treat your burger like a steak. Sear it beautifully on both sides, then let it rest and it will continue to cook to medium. If you cook it to medium and then let it rest, it will be very dry.

SERVES 4

ONION RELISH
2 red onions, finely sliced / 50g butter / 1 tablespoon demerara sugar / 1 tablespoon balsamic vinegar

1 large red onion, peeled and finely chopped / 1kg minced lean beef / sea salt and freshly ground black pepper / vegetable oil / butter / 4 large burger baps, toasted / 4 large pickled gherkins, sliced / 2 beef tomatoes, sliced / 1 baby gem lettuce, washed and divided / shavings of Parmesan cheese / chips, for serving (see page 241)

To make the onion relish, fry the onions in the butter until soft. Add the sugar to the pan and fry for a further 4–5 minutes until caramelized. Drain the excess fat from the pan and add the balsamic vinegar. Cook for 2–3 minutes more until it has the consistency of a syrup. Put aside until ready to use.

Mix the chopped onion into the minced beef and season well. Mould the mince into 4 large balls and press down lightly to shape them into burgers, then leave them to set in the fridge for a couple of hours.

When you're ready to cook the burgers, get a large frying pan or griddle pan hot, and cook them in a little vegetable oil for 10–15 minutes. This will cook them medium, so adjust the timing depending on whether you like your burger a bit rarer or slightly more well done. Add a little butter to the pan towards the end of the cooking time.

Serve the burgers straight away on the toasted baps with the salad garnishes and Parmesan on top and the chips on the side. Top with the onion relish.

COTTAGE PIE

This has to be my all-time favourite comfort food dish. My wife, Tana, and I go out and have dinner once a week by ourselves. We usually go to the Ivy and I always order the same thing – Caesar salad and cottage pie. The waiters there think I'm so boring because I always have the same, but I just love it. I'll sit there with a dinky bottle of ketchup and one of Worcestershire sauce and that is just it for me. Nothing more, nothing else, just my cottage pie. A quick tip for this dish is not to allow your mashed potato to become too watery, so use Desiree potatoes, which work best here.

SERVES 4

olive oil / sea salt and freshly ground black pepper / 900g minced lean beef / 450g onions, peeled and finely chopped / 2 cloves of garlic / 2 sprigs of fresh thyme, leaves picked and chopped / 2 tablespoons tomato purée / 25g flour / 200ml red wine / 75ml Worcestershire sauce / 1 litre brown chicken stock (see page 237) / 1kg Desiree potatoes, peeled and halved / 2 egg yolks

Preheat the oven to 200°C/400°F/gas 6. Heat some oil in a large pan until smoking hot. Season the mince and fry, in batches if necessary. Once cooked, drain off the fat using a sieve. In a second large pan, fry the onions, garlic and thyme until soft and golden. Add the meat and the tomato purée and sprinkle with the flour. Stir constantly for a few minutes to cook the flour, then add the red wine and Worcestershire sauce and continue to cook until the liquid has reduced by half. Add the stock and bring to the boil, then turn the heat down and simmer for 30–40 minutes. By this time the mixture should be thick and glossy.

Meanwhile, cook your potatoes in salted boiling water until tender. Mash them, then beat in the egg yolks. Remove the mince from the heat, allow to cool slightly and check the seasoning. Add some more Worcestershire sauce – in my opinion the more the better! Either divide the meat between individual serving dishes or use one large dish, and pipe or fork the mash over the top. Bake in the oven for about 30 minutes until bubbling and golden brown.

LASAGNE

This is a modern version of lasagne taken to a different level — it's a way of revitalizing something that we have allowed to become boring. If you have never tried making your own pasta sheets before, it is definitely worth having a go. They're great fun to do when you're with the kids, so let them help you out. If you can, it's best to make the sheets the day before you need them and dry them overnight. If not, then start them a couple of hours before you begin cooking. For this lasagne I use slices of beef fillet rather than the more traditional minced beef, and rather than baking it at the end I build it up on the plate layer by layer.

SERVES 4
4 tablespoons crème fraîche / 2 egg yolks / 50g grated Parmesan cheese / 600g good beef fillet / olive oil / 2 large shallots, chopped / 1 clove of garlic /500g cherry tomatoes, halved / 8 slices of Parma ham

PASTA DOUGH
275g pasta flour / 2 whole eggs / 3 egg yolks / a pinch of salt / olive oil

Mix all the pasta ingredients together in a food processor until they form a dough, then knead it for about 15 minutes on a floured surface until it is smooth. Put it to one side and let it rest for 1–2 hours.

When the dough has rested, roll it out into thin sheets. Cut these sheets into 8 squares about 15 x 15cm. Blanch the squares in boiling salted water for about 10 seconds and then refresh in iced water and pat dry. (Any pasta dough left over will keep for 1 day in the refrigerator, wrapped in clingfilm. Use it to make other pasta — tagliatelle, pappardelle and so on.) Lay the pasta squares on a baking sheet. Mix the crème fraîche and egg yolks together and then spoon this mixture over the pasta squares. Sprinkle with Parmesan and place under a very hot grill until glazed and bubbling.

Meanwhile, cut the beef into four portions and fry in a little olive oil until medium rare — 7–10 minutes. In a separate pan, sauté the shallots and garlic in more olive oil and add the tomatoes. Cook quickly for about 5 minutes so that the tomatoes start to just break down.

Serve on flat plates, as follows. First lay out a slice of Parma ham and top with a spoon of tomato mix. Slice each portion of beef into about 8 slices and place half of them on top of each spoonful of tomato mix. Then top with a sheet of pasta. Repeat this process again so you end up with a 'stack' of lasagne. Drizzle with olive oil and serve straight away.

LAMB STEW WITH PARSLEY DUMPLINGS
AND YOUNG CARROTS

This is a dish I grew up with — not because it was a luxurious treat in my family but because it was fairly cheap to make. Lamb neck, like the shank, has a high fat content running through it, so the longer you cook it the more tender it becomes. It's a nice way of introducing kids to something quite robust. I would never serve best end of lamb to them while they're young, but lamb neck is fine as it's stewed for a long time. I've introduced this dish to a few of the outlets we've worked on in the television series because it can be put together in the morning and then slowly braised for a few hours while you get on with other things. If you want a quicker cooking time at home, cut the cubes of meat smaller and cook the stew for 45 minutes. But I like big chunky pieces of meat, so I prefer to cook it for longer.

SERVES 4
sea salt and freshly ground black pepper / 750g lamb neck, cut into large pieces / 1 tablespoon flour / olive oil / 3 tablespoons tomato purée / 1 clove of garlic, lightly crushed / a sprig of fresh thyme / 1 bay leaf / 1 litre brown chicken stock (see page 237) or lamb stock / 2 bunches of young carrots

DUMPLINGS
115g plain flour / 55g suet / 3 tablespoons chopped flat-leaf parsley / sea salt and freshly ground black pepper / optional: good chicken stock

Season the lamb pieces and dust with the flour. Heat some olive oil in a large pan and colour them all over. Pour off any excess oil, add the tomato purée, and cook for a further 2–3 minutes before adding the garlic, herbs and stock. Bring to the boil, then turn the heat down and simmer for 1½–2 hours until tender. Towards the end of the cooking time, peel the carrots and cook in boiling salted water until tender.

To make the dumplings, mix the flour, suet, parsley and seasoning with enough cold water to make a soft dough. Divide into small balls. Heat the chicken stock or water in a separate pan and poach the dumplings for 10–15 minutes until soft and puffed up.

When the lamb is cooked, remove it from the pan and pass the sauce through a sieve. Pour the sauce back into the pan with the lamb, carrots and dumplings and return to the heat for everything to warm through. Serve immediately.

PHEASANT BAKED WITH CÈPES

The secret to this dish is the fresh cèpes – but if you can't get hold of any, then use dried ones instead. We do have access to the most amazing wild cèpes in this country now though – from the New Forest, to Romsey, to Southampton. There is a real secrecy among the chefs who go mushroom-picking – because the mushrooms are free and they are amazing. So they keep it to themselves about where to go picking. To give you an idea of how much cèpes cost, for fresh South African ones we can expect to pay about £25 per kilo, and the French ones are more expensive! The second alternative is to use a beautiful girolle mushroom. I don't like to peel them as I don't want any waste, so I gently scrub them with a toothbrush. If you don't want the traditional mash with this, lots of baked beetroot is good. Or mashed celeriac with olive oil and some chopped fresh rosemary is a nice alternative.

SERVES 4

85g fresh cèpes / sea salt and freshly ground black pepper / 1–2 large pheasants / 115g butter / 255ml white wine / 2 cloves of garlic, chopped / 500ml good chicken stock / 1 tablespoon plain flour / 2 tablespoons chopped flat-leaf parsley / mashed potato, to serve (see page 241)

Preheat the oven to 180°C/350°F/gas 4. Chop the cèpes into even-sized pieces. Season the pheasants. Melt 85g of the butter in a roasting pan and fry the pheasants until golden all over. Add the wine, garlic and chicken stock. Put the roasting pan in the oven and cook the pheasants for about 20 minutes on each side, then remove the birds and keep warm. Boil the remaining cooking liquor until it has reduced by half.

Meanwhile, sauté the cèpes in the remaining butter for about 10 minutes until golden. Sprinkle over the flour and continue to cook for 3 minutes, then add the reduced cooking liquor and simmer for 15 minutes to make a smooth sauce. Stir in the parsley. Pour the sauce over the pheasants and serve with mashed potato.

VENISON PIE

In the ingredients list I've suggested venison casserole meat — the best cut for this would be the leg. This is a vibrant, earthy, rustic pie enhanced with pancetta. There are a lot of vegetables here which we use in this country — I really adore swede. And then some classic pastry to top it. It's worth knowing that you can add texture to the pie by tossing the meat in seasoned flour before cooking. This acts as a thickening agent. This is a seasonal September to March pie, but if you want to make it in summer then use a large capon chicken. It's quite rich and classy made with pork, too — just follow the same method. There was a venison stew on the menu at the Walnut Tree that was rather insipid, so I reworked it and made it into a pie.

SERVES 4

20g dried cèpes / 6 tablespoons olive oil / 100g pancetta or smoked bacon / 1 red onion, peeled and chopped / 2 cloves of garlic, peeled and chopped / 1 large carrot, peeled and finely chopped / 1 stick of celery, trimmed and finely chopped / 1 small swede, peeled and finely chopped / 600g venison casserole meat / sea salt and freshly ground black pepper / flour for dusting / 3 tablespoons sherry vinegar / 200ml red wine / 1 tablespoon juniper berries, crushed / 2 bay leaves / 350g puff pastry / 1 egg yolk, beaten

Preheat the oven to 200°C/400°F/gas 6. Put the cèpes in a bowl and pour over 600ml of boiling water. Leave to cool. Heat the olive oil in a frying pan and sauté the pancetta or bacon until brown. Add the onion and garlic and continue to cook until golden brown. Add all the other vegetables to the pan and cook until soft, then transfer everything into a casserole dish. Toss the meat in a little seasoned flour and fry until browned, then add to the casserole with the vinegar, the wine, the cèpes and their strained soaking liquid. Bring to the boil, then add the juniper berries and season. Add the bay leaves, cover, and cook for 1½ hours in the preheated oven until the meat is tender.

Roll out the puff pastry and cut out a round to fit the casserole dish. Place it over the dish, then brush with the beaten egg yolk and bake in the preheated oven for about 15 minutes until the pastry is golden and crisp.

BANG BANG CHICKEN

Bang Bang chicken is a dish that originates from China. On a Friday night I go to one of my favourite Chinese restaurants, Memories of China, with all my head chefs to have a chill-out and some fun. And that's how we became familiar with this dish. Normally when you get smoked meat it's watery or too plastic, but Mr But from the restaurant tea-smokes his chicken breast and then when it cools he covers it with the lovely Bang Bang sauce. It's a perfect starter with crispy lettuce. And always good to eat while having conversation. Use smooth peanut butter — if you haven't any, you can heat up the crunchy type and blitz it. It's a very quick dish to put together because you can buy smoked chicken breasts from any good deli, and then all you have to do is assemble the salad ingredients.

SERVES 4
1 baby gem lettuce, washed / 4 smoked chicken breasts, thickly sliced / 1 carrot, peeled and julienned / 3 spring onions, trimmed and julienned / 1 red onion, peeled and julienned / 4 teaspoons sesame seeds, lightly toasted

SAUCE
250g smooth peanut butter / 5 teaspoons sweet chilli sauce / 5 tablespoons sesame oil / 6 tablespoons vegetable oil

Whisk together the sauce ingredients in a heatproof bowl and warm them gently over simmering water in a saucepan or bain-marie (see page 244). This should only take a matter of minutes.

Meanwhile, separate the baby gem lettuce leaves and lay them on a large plate with the chicken slices over the top. Scatter the julienned vegetables round the chicken and spoon over the warm sauce. Sprinkle with the toasted sesame seeds and serve immediately, letting everyone help themselves.

MARINATED DUCK BREASTS

When I was at the Walnut Tree I saw that they had a very grey, very insipid salted duck dish on the menu. They hadn't properly cured it or removed the salt, and the meat had been poached. This way of cooking doesn't release the fat, so we decided to pan-roast it and caramelize the fat to make it tasty. If you then roll the duck in foil and put it in the fridge, it will be ready to serve the next day. Lovely with a blood orange salad – segment your orange and then drizzle with a touch of classic vinaigrette (see page 217) and rip over some fresh basil leaves.

SERVES 4
2 duck breasts / 50g sea salt / 4 star anise, broken up / 10 coriander seeds / zest of 1 orange and 1 lemon / 1 clove of garlic, quartered / freshly ground black pepper / olive oil

Score the duck breasts with a knife, then sprinkle with sea salt, star anise, coriander seeds, the orange and lemon zest and the garlic. Put them in between two trays, weighted down, so that the salt and flavourings penetrate the meat. The salt will remove moisture and cure the duck. You will need to let the duck breasts sit for an hour or more so that they part marinate, part cure. Shake off all the flavourings, then rinse well to wash off all the salt.

Heat a little olive oil in a frying pan and fry the duck breasts skin side down over a high heat for 2 minutes until golden brown. Turn the breasts over to seal them for 1 minute.

Take the duck breasts off the heat and place on a rack to cool, letting the juices drain off. Roll them up in foil. Leave in the fridge to chill for at least 24 hours, then unwrap the foil and dry the duck breasts with kitchen paper. They are now ready to be sliced and served.

'A study in pork' — what the hell does that mean? Well, I'll tell you what it means to the hotel dining room that included it on its menu: six individual pork meals in miniature displayed on one oblong plate. Everything from the traditional English breakfast with pork sausage to Szechuan minced pork dim sum and roast belly pork. What a travesty.

It's crucial to be clear on the style of food you're serving and to stick to your identity. Only use French on your menu if you're confident that you're describing a cooking term (as opposed to translating every dish into French to make it sound exotic). On one menu I saw 'Eventail de melon rafraîchi', which was really just a fan of melon. Never ever use Franglais, as in 'Poulet korma' or 'Mousse de legumes multi-colour'. The research team on *Ramsay's Kitchen Nightmares* spotted the 'hidden prawn cocktail' on nearly half the 700 menus they were sent from restaurants around the country. What's wrong with calling a prawn cocktail a prawn cocktail? Forget 'Crevettes nestling on a bed of chiffonade lettuce in a Marie Rose sauce' or 'Melody of juicy prawns and shrimps bound with spicy mayonnaise and mixed leaves'.

I hate a menu that has the audacity to say 'All our meat is cooked pink.' If you've got a beautiful rack of lamb or Barbary duck breast, you may not choose to eat that dish well done yourself, but that's the customer's prerogative. The minute you think you're more important than the customers you might as well kiss them goodbye.

In other words, food should speak for itself — keep the menu simple and straightforward and cut out the waffle. Why on earth would you put, 'If our freezer breaks down, don't worry, it's only chips and ice cream off the menu'? There's no point admitting your weaknesses to your customers as they did at the Glass House. And if you've recently invested in a laminating machine, give it to your local charity shop. The laminated menu has to be the worst thing that's happened to restaurant-menu design in the past ten years.

puddings

'Pudding is a great way to treat yourself. You go into a restaurant sometimes and you look at the menu and you think, "Wow, I so deserve that"'

My wife Tana's biggest frustration when we go out to eat is that by the time we get to the pudding I'm never hungry – because as a chef I tend to pick at food all day long. I can manage a starter and a main course, but I can never eat pudding. Which is a real shame, because pudding is the grande finale, the point where the whole experience becomes upbeat and vibrant and you have a great end to the most perfect dinner.

I've found that a lot of customers will pick their pudding before they choose the starter and main course. All this bumf about how bad puddings are for you – well, in moderation they aren't bad at all. Of course, if you take them in quantum leaps that's a different matter!

One of my favourite puddings from my time spent working in Paris is the Calvados rice pudding with caramelized apples. And the apple and cardamom tarte Tatin with cardamom ice cream is amazing. Of course you might not want to make cardamom-flavoured ice cream – vanilla, or even crème fraîche, is just as nice. Cold chocolate mousse is something we bargain with our kids over, as a treat for a Saturday or Sunday lunch. Black Forest gateau is a very retro pudding, probably the most bastardized pudding in Britain, made famous in the seventies and starting to creep back on to menus all across the country. We serve it at the Boxwood Café, and if it's done to perfection and you've got the right kind of fresh cherries and good rich chocolate, it's to die for.

Puddings are a great social event. When I go out to dinner with a group of friends, it's the only course where everyone will tend to taste a bit of everyone else's. If I'm to give you a final tip, it's that you should always try to save some room for pudding.

MINT CRÈME BRÛLÉE WITH STRAWBERRIES

The secret of a perfect crème brûlée is never to use coarse demerara sugar. Always use a fine one – you want to get a discreet layer of caramel, not one that is a centimetre thick. There is nothing worse than seeing customers crashing their spoons against a dense layer of caramel. If you've only got coarse sugar at home, put it in the blender to make it finer. You can even dust your brûlées with icing sugar as an alternative – this works beautifully as well. It's important never to over-burn or blacken the caramel, as the last thing you want is to have a thick, bitter caramel set against a nice mellow cream. Apart from worrying about what it's doing to your teeth, it's just not good to eat. I recommend you get yourself a blowtorch for use in the kitchen – you can buy small ones now which are a bit like cigar lighters.

SERVES 4
350ml double cream / 125ml whole milk / 1 bunch of fresh mint / 6 large eggs / 75g caster sugar / 4 tablespoons fine demerara sugar, for dusting / a handful of strawberries

Preheat the oven to 140°C/275°F/gas 1. Put the cream and milk into a saucepan, together with the mint. Bring to the boil, then remove from the heat and put to one side to infuse for 2 hours. Whisk the eggs and caster sugar until creamy. Bring the milk back to the boil, then pass through a sieve into the egg mixture. Strain again and divide between four small dishes. Bake for about 40 minutes then remove from the oven. When cool, refrigerate for at least an hour.

Just before serving, dust the top of each brûlée with 1 tablespoon of demerara sugar and glaze with a blowtorch. Serve with a few strawberries on top of each brûlée.

CARAMELIZED PINEAPPLE WITH SHERBET

This recipe is ideal for using up every single part of a pineapple, including the core. If you are able to get hold of a sweet pineapple to start with, you won't need to add the syrup to it. Be generous when topping the pineapple with the yoghurt, as the freshness of it goes so well with the bittersweet fruit. We tend to serve this in my restaurants as a pre-dessert and it's one of the most popular things on the menu.

SERVES 4
1 large pineapple, peeled / 175g caster sugar / 250ml water / 300g Greek yoghurt

Purée the pineapple in a blender until pulpy. Spread a large muslin cloth on the worktop and put the puréed pineapple in the centre. Gather the corners of the cloth together and hang up over a bowl to catch the juice.

Put 75g of the sugar in a pan with the water. Bring to the boil, then simmer for 5 minutes to make a sugar syrup. When all the pineapple juice has dripped through the muslin, mix it with the syrup and freeze in a suitable container.

In a large heavy-bottomed pan, heat the remaining sugar gently until it is caramelized. Add the pineapple pulp and cook until the caramel has dissolved. Leave to cool. When ready to serve, take the frozen pineapple sherbet out of the freezer. Divide the pineapple mixture between four glasses. Top with the yoghurt and scrape some frozen pineapple shavings on top.

BANANA SOUFFLÉS

Most of this pudding is made up of banana purée. It's quite important to cook out all the alcohol from it to drive out any moisture that occurs naturally in the ingredients. You want to end up with a really thick, firm purée, because if any liquid remains it will break down the egg whites and the soufflés won't rise.

BANANA PURÉE
400g bananas / 150g crème de banane

CRÈME PATISSIÈRE
375ml milk / 1 vanilla pod / 3 egg yolks / 75g sugar / 50g flour / 40g butter

TO MAKE 4 SOUFFLÉS
400g banana purée (see above) / 120g crème patissière (see above) / 400g egg white (about 10 egg whites) / 140g caster sugar, plus a little for the dishes / softened butter for the dishes

To make the banana purée, blitz the bananas in a liquidizer until very smooth. Put the crème de banane in a pan and heat gently for 2–3 minutes until it has a syrupy consistency. Add the puréed banana and cook for a further 3–4 minutes, then remove from the pan and pass through a fine sieve.

To make the crème patissière, put the milk into a small pan. Split the vanilla pod lengthways, scrape out the seeds, and add both the pod and the seeds to the milk. Bring to the boil, then turn off the heat and leave to infuse for 10 minutes. Remove the vanilla pod, squeezing it to ensure all the lovely stickiness is left in the milk. In a large bowl whisk the egg yolks and sugar until the mixture is thick and pale, then add the flour. Return the milk to the heat. As it comes up to the boil, strain a couple of spoonfuls of the hot milk on to the egg yolk mixture and whisk it in. Then pour in the rest of the strained milk and whisk until smooth. Clean the pan out, then pour the mixture back into the pan and heat gently, stirring constantly with a whisk, until it just starts to bubble. Continue to cook for 3–4 minutes, whisking all the time. Remove from the heat and whisk in the butter, then set aside to cool.

To make the soufflés, whisk the banana purée and the crème patissière together in a large bowl. Allow the mixture to cool to room temperature. In a clean bowl, whisk the egg whites until they just start to form soft peaks. Then sprinkle in the sugar and continue whisking until the egg whites form slightly firmer peaks. Gently beat a small amount of the egg whites into the soufflé mixture to loosen it up again. In two further batches, softly fold the rest of the egg white into the mixture. This is so you don't lose any air.

(continued overleaf)

Preheat the oven to 170°C/325°F/gas 3. Grease 4 soufflé dishes with softened butter and put in the fridge for about 10 minutes to set. Once set, sprinkle some caster sugar all around the moulds so it's evenly distributed. This will prevent the soufflés sticking to the sides of the dishes and help them rise nicely. Fill the dishes to the top with the soufflé mixture, then take a palette knife and flatten off the surface. Pass your thumb round the edges of the moulds to remove any mixture that has run over the sides, as this can get too crisp and will stop the soufflés from rising. Put the soufflés into the preheated oven and cook for 10–12 minutes. Don't keep opening the oven to look at them, as this lets the heat out and the soufflés may not rise. When they are risen and golden on top, take out and serve hot. Lovely with a toffee-flavoured ice cream.

BANANA STICKY TOFFEE PUDDING

This is a real old-fashioned favourite. Usually it's made with sultanas, but we've created a really modern twist by using bananas. Steam or bake the mixture in moulds in a bain-marie (see page 244). Best served with a sweet sticky toffee sauce. This pudding is also lovely with fresh custard or crème fraîche.

SERVES 4
170g unsalted butter / 180g soft brown sugar / 2 small eggs / 180g plain flour / 12g baking powder / 200g chopped banana / butter and caster sugar for the moulds

TOFFEE SAUCE
250g soft brown sugar / 140ml double cream / 65g unsalted butter

Preheat the oven to 180°C/350°F/gas 4. Cream the butter and the sugar together in a large bowl, then slowly beat in the eggs. Gently fold in the sieved flour and baking powder, then mix in the chopped banana. Grease 6 baking moulds with a little butter and a sprinkling of caster sugar. Divide the mixture between the moulds, until each one is three-quarters full. Bake for 10 minutes, then turn the heat down to 150°C/300°F/gas 2 and cook for a further 1 hour and 20 minutes.

While the puddings are cooking, make your toffee sauce. Place the sugar, cream and butter in a pan and bring to the boil. When all the sugar has dissolved, remove from the heat. Remove the puddings from the oven and leave to rest, then turn out of the moulds and serve topped with the toffee sauce.

CHOCOLATE AND TOFFEE FONDANT

We borrowed this recipe from one of my restaurants, the Boxwood Café, to put on the menu at the Glass House. It's a light chocolate sponge with a lovely liquid centre. Just wonderful when you break into it with your spoon. I've enhanced the recipe by making a toffee fondant and adding that to the sponge. Delicious served with chocolate sauce and vanilla ice cream.

SERVES 4
butter and flour for moulds / 200g butter / 100g flour / 4 whole eggs / 4 egg yolks / 250g sugar / 200g bitter chocolate (at least 70% cocoa solids)

TOFFEE FONDANT
250g sugar / 200ml double cream

Preheat the oven to 180°C/350°F/gas 4. To make the toffee fondant, put 30g of the sugar in a pan with 2 tablespoons of water and bring to the boil. Simmer for 5 minutes to make a sugar syrup, then remove from the heat. Put the remaining sugar in a large pan and add the sugar syrup. Heat to 120°C/235°F, then slowly add half the cream and cook until the mixture is golden brown. Beat in the remaining cream and leave to cool. Refrigerate for an hour or so, until set.

Line your serving moulds with a little butter, then dust with flour and put them in the fridge for 10 minutes for the butter to set. Meanwhile, whisk the eggs, yolks and sugar in a large bowl until light and fluffy. Melt the chocolate and butter in a bowl over hot water. Mix the flour into the egg mixture, then fold in the chocolate.

Fill the moulds two-thirds of the way up with the sponge mix, then take half a tablespoon of the toffee fondant mixture and place it in the centre. Place a little more of the sponge mix on top to cover the toffee. Bake in the oven for 10–15 minutes until set. Leave to rest for 3–4 minutes, then pat out of the moulds and serve straight away.

APPLE AND CARDAMOM TARTE TATIN WITH CARDAMOM ICE CREAM

This is a recipe for a classic apple tarte Tatin, but with a twist. I decided to experiment with it, using cardamom seeds in both the tart and the ice cream. Cardamom is mostly used in Indian cooking, so you might not think that it would work well in a sweet dessert. However, it has a lovely floral flavour to it, like a burst of flowers in your mouth. I tried cracking some cardamom seeds into the sugar and butter mixture before caramelizing the apples and it really worked well.

SERVES 2
3 large Braeburn apples / 300g puff pastry / 50g unsalted butter, thinly sliced / 50g caster sugar / 5 cardamom pods, crushed

ICE CREAM
250ml milk / 250ml double cream / 10 cardamom pods, crushed / 6 egg yolks / 90g caster sugar

Peel, core and quarter the apples, then leave to dry uncovered for 2–3 hours. (Don't worry if they go a bit brown.)

To make the ice cream, put the milk, cream and cardamom pods in a large pan and bring to the boil, then turn off the heat and leave to infuse for an hour. Whisk the egg yolks and sugar together in a bowl, then pour the milk mixture over the top and whisk again. Transfer to a thick-bottomed pan and cook gently until the mixture will coat the back of a spoon. Leave to cool, then pass through a sieve and churn in an ice cream machine until smooth.

Preheat the oven to 200°C/400°F/gas 6. Roll out the pastry and cut a circle 24cm in diameter. Spread the butter over the bottom of a shallow pan that will also go in the oven, and sprinkle over the sugar. Dot the cardamom pods over the top and press the apple quarters into the butter to make a circle, with one quarter in the centre. Place the pan over a medium heat until the butter and sugar dissolve and a light caramel forms. Remove from the heat and chill. Lay the pastry on top of the apples and tuck down the sides so that it touches the bottom of the pan. Place the pan in the preheated oven and bake for 15–20 minutes until the pastry is very crisp. Remove from the oven and leave to cool.

Turn out on to a serving plate and serve with a scoop of the ice cream.

COLD CHOCOLATE MOUSSE WITH
LAVENDER ICE CREAM

This chocolate mousse is thick and unctuous with real body to it but at the same time is quite light. This is the main difference between this mousse and the usual chocolate mousse, which tends to be all air with no body at all.

Infusing lavender into the milk makes a lovely ice cream. The combination of lavender and chocolate, for some reason, just goes really well together. It's a nice, refreshing ice cream to have with the richness of the chocolate.

SERVES 4
275g caster sugar / 5 egg yolks / 1 teaspoon liquid glucose (available from chemists and cake-decorating shops) / 2 large egg whites / 200g Valrhona dark chocolate (70% cocoa solids) / 300ml double cream

ICE CREAM
250ml milk / 250ml double cream / a good handful of fresh lavender flowers, plus extra for sprinkling / 6 egg yolks / 90g caster sugar

Make the ice cream first. Bring the milk, cream and handful of lavender flowers to the boil, then turn the heat down and leave to infuse for an hour. Whisk the egg yolks and sugar together, then pour the milk mixture over the top and whisk again. Transfer to a thick-bottomed pan and cook gently until the mixture will coat the back of a spoon. Leave to cool, then pass through a sieve and churn in an ice cream machine until smooth.

In a heavy-bottomed pan heat 100ml of water and 150g of the caster sugar to 120°C/235°F. Meanwhile, whisk the yolks with a hand-held electric whisk until pale and frothy. Slowly pour on the hot sugar liquid, beating continuously until cold and very thick.

Mix the remaining caster sugar into a heavy-bottomed pan with the glucose and 2 table-spoons of water and bring to the boil. Whisk the egg whites until soft peaks begin to form. Slowly add the hot sugar syrup, whisking until the whites are cold, thick and shiny.

Gently melt the chocolate in a bowl over hot water, then cool slightly and fold into the egg whites. Mix with the sugar and egg yolk mixture. Whip the cream until thick and fold into the mixture. Pipe or spoon the mousse into glasses and top with a ball of lavender ice cream. Lovely sprinkled with the extra lavender flowers.

CALVADOS RICE PUDDING WITH
CARAMELIZED APPLES

Rice puddings are usually baked in the oven and they end up with a really horrible crust and overcooked nuggets of rice. However, the rice in this recipe is cooked nice and slowly in milk flavoured with vanilla. We then bring it together at the end by adding the whisked egg yolks and sugar to give it a light finish but with more volume. So when you're eating it, it's really thick and creamy but not heavy. It makes a really great combination with the caramelized apples on top.

SERVES 4
300ml milk / 300ml double cream / 1 vanilla pod / 150g pudding rice / 6 egg yolks / 250g caster sugar / 50ml Calvados / 50g butter / 3 large Braeburn apples, peeled

Put the milk, cream and vanilla pod into a large pan, bring to the boil, then turn off the heat and leave to infuse for about 10 minutes. Add the rice and bring to a simmer, then continue to cook, stirring occasionally, for about 20 minutes until the rice is soft and the liquid almost gone.

In a bowl whisk the egg yolks and 150g of the caster sugar until light and fluffy and pour into the rice. Cook gently for about 5 minutes until thick and creamy, then leave to cool slightly. Stir in the Calvados.

Meanwhile, put the remaining caster sugar in a heavy-bottomed pan with 1 tablespoon of water, and heat gently until the sugar caramelizes. Mix in the butter. Using a melon baller, scoop out rounds from the peeled apples and drop into the caramel. Cook for 5–6 minutes until golden brown, then scatter over the rice pudding.

BLACK FOREST GATEAU

Although I've stuck to the chocolate sponge and black cherry combination, I've rein-vented this classic by using a pannacotta mix to spread inside instead of whipped cream.

SERVES 4

KIRSCH PANNACOTTA
565ml cream / 140ml milk / 100g sugar / 2 leaves of gelatine / 25ml kirsch

CHOCOLATE MOUSSE
50g sugar / 45ml water / 2 egg yolks / 180ml cream / 25ml milk / 100g bitter chocolate (70% cocoa solids)

CHOCOLATE SPONGE
8 eggs / 250g sugar / 200g soft flour / 50g cocoa powder

CHERRY COMPOTE
200g black cherries / 50g sugar / 50ml kirsch

TO DECORATE
whipped cream and shavings of chocolate

To make the kirsch pannacotta, put the cream, milk and sugar into a pan and bring to the boil. Soften the gelatine in water and stir into the cream mixture. Transfer to a bowl and add the kirsch. Chill the mixture in the fridge.

To make the chocolate mousse, heat the sugar and water in a pan to 120°C/235°F to form a sugar syrup. Whisk the egg yolks until pale, then gradually whisk in the syrup and continue whisking until the mixture thickens. Whip the cream and the milk together until thickened but still floppy. Melt the chocolate in a bowl over simmering water. Add a little of the cream mixture to it and whisk, then fold in the rest of the cream and chill.

To make the chocolate sponge, first preheat the oven to 180°C/350°F/gas 4. Whisk the eggs and sugar until pale and fluffy, then fold in the sieved flour and cocoa powder. Pour into a greased and lined cake tin and cook in the preheated oven for 15 minutes. Remove from the oven and leave to cool.

To make the cherry compote, put the cherries and sugar in a pan over a gentle heat until all the sugar has dissolved. Add the kirsch and leave to cool.

When the sponge cake has cooled, split it horizontally into three layers. Spread the bottom layer with the pannacotta mix and put the middle layer of sponge on top. Spread this layer with the chocolate mousse, followed by the cherry compote, and top with the third layer of sponge. Spread the cherry compote over the top, followed by a layer of whipped cream and some chocolate shavings.

PEAR FINANCIER

This is a pear sponge cake in which I've used a lot of browned butter to give the sponge a nutty taste. One great thing about this pudding is that you can make it in the morning and at dinnertime it'll still taste fresh. It's very light, and delicious with poached pears. Serve with crème fraîche, sprinkled with chopped mint.

SERVES 4

125g unsalted butter / 4 pears / 165g caster sugar / 25g plain flour / 125g ground almonds / 160g egg whites (about 4 egg whites)

Preheat the oven to 190°C/375°F/gas 5. Put the butter in a pan over a high heat and cook until it starts to go brown. Strain through a fine sieve and leave to cool. Peel and core the pears and chop into 1cm dice. Put 75g of the caster sugar into a warmed pan and heat gently until caramelized. Add the diced pear and cook for about 4–5 minutes, until it just starts to break down. Take out of the pan and leave to cool on a tray.

Mix the flour, the ground almonds and the remaining sugar in a large bowl. Slowly fold in the egg whites, then stir in the melted butter. Grease six moulds or ramekins with butter, and dust with a little flour. Put in the fridge for 10 minutes for the butter to set. Combine the almond mixture with the pears, then pour into the moulds until three-quarters full. Bake at the top of the preheated oven for 25 minutes until golden brown and firm.

Also nice with peaches.

WHISKY BREAD AND BUTTER PUDDING

The idea behind this recipe is to use nice light panettone, sliced up, which makes a lovely light pudding. The panettone is then flavoured with a creamy custard and either whisky or Baileys, and layered between the slices are prunes. Lovely!

SERVES 4

50g butter, softened / 150g panettone, sliced / 60g prunes, stoned and halved / 2 large egg yolks / 2 large eggs / 40g caster sugar / 300ml double cream / 300ml milk / 4 tablespoons whisky or Baileys / demerara sugar to sprinkle / 3 tablespoons apricot jam

Grease a 1.5 litre ovenproof dish with a little of the butter, then spread the rest over the panettone slices. Place the bread in a bowl, sprinkling over the prunes. Beat the yolks and whole eggs together with the sugar in another bowl until creamy, then add the cream, milk and whisky or Baileys. Pour this mixture over the bread and using your hands gently knead it all together. Leave for about 20 minutes to allow the bread to soak up the custard.

Place the bread slices in the ovenproof dish, layering them with the prunes. Then shake over some demerara sugar. Place the dish in a bain-marie (see page 244) and bake at 180°C/350°F/gas 4 for 40–50 minutes until golden. Warm the apricot jam until runny, and when the pudding is cooked brush the top with the jam. Leave to stand for 15 minutes before serving.

It's always nice to have the kitchen functioning round the clock. At night it's possible to get all the stuff done that you can't really do during the day: preparing all the dried fruit, the breads, the ice creams and crème brûlées. It's the most perfect time to make things because it's quiet. But also, at that time of the night the kitchen has an even temperature throughout, which is great, for instance, if you're making a special bread.

I've always enjoyed working on my own. When I was twenty-two I was on the bakery section at Le Gavroche — my shift would run from midnight to midday, and it was absolutely full on. The work schedule, the plan, was staggering, and I had to follow it to the tee. It detailed specifically what I had to do at midnight, or at 12.30 a.m. It had things on it like: 'At 0130 take the butter out of the fridge for half an hour to get it soft.' It was always such a tight schedule and there was absolutely no room for error. But it was a great experience.

We had all these beautiful little yeast fermentations going on, and it was just amazing, absolutely amazing. I really had to move my arse, I had so much to do: all the dough was hand-rolled, all hand-cut. I'd knock back the brioche, make sourdough, walnut and raisin bread, tomato bread. I loved doing it so much that once I finished at midday I would want to go on to a section and do lunch, or just help someone out, but in that type of kitchen they just wanted you to go home and get some rest so you were ready for the next night shift.

vinaigrettes & dressings

'The great thing about vinaigrettes and dressings is that they're so versatile and they can reflect the seasons in their flavours'

Over the last five years there has been a general move away from using heavy, seductive, rich sauces made from cream, butter and things like veal stock in my kitchens. We've tended to lighten everything up, and by doing this we have introduced lots of fish dishes, meats and salads that have been finished off with vinaigrettes and dressings instead.

Vinaigrettes and dressings are fresh and fragrant with things like orange and lime zest throughout the summer, and then everything becomes a little bit heavier with rustic herbs — thyme, rosemary and garlic oil — during the winter. Vinaigrette can also be used to cut through the richness of a sauce. For instance, in my restaurant kitchens now, instead of saucing a dish completely the chefs will use just half the amount of sauce and finish it off with a vinaigrette. And we're also starting to glaze a lot more fish and meat with vinaigrette now, as opposed to using a sauce.

I always like to add three or four tablespoons of water to my vinaigrettes when I'm using virgin olive oil. This makes them less cloying and less heavy on the palate. What I've done in this chapter is to give you the basic classic vinaigrette which I use a lot. Different flavourings can be added to take it in various directions — whether it's with some mustard or lemon grass, chillies, rosemary or confit of lemon.

CLASSIC VINAIGRETTE

This vinaigrette is incredibly versatile. It can be used for dressing salads, braising glazed fish and marinating cooked potatoes. We use it in our restaurants in most of our main dishes to cut through the sauces and lighten them up. Keeps for 1 week in the fridge or larder — shake well each time you use it. Makes 800ml.

600ml good olive oil / 200ml white wine vinegar / sea salt and freshly ground black pepper

This is incredibly simple to make. Place all three ingredients into a bowl and emulsify with a hand blender.

À LA GRECQUE

'À la Grecque' in French means 'in the Greek manner', and describes a method of cooking vegetables in a mixture of oil and vinegar or lemon juice. This vinaigrette is wonderful to marinate boiled potatoes in. Put in a bowl, add the cooked and drained potatoes, and leave them overnight. The potatoes will soak up the dressing and be absolutely delicious to eat the next day, hot or cold. This vinaigrette has no shelf life — you need to make it and use it straight away because of the fresh herbs. Makes 400ml.

300ml olive oil / 100ml white wine vinegar / a sprig of fresh thyme / a few sprigs of fresh basil / 25 coriander seeds / 5 star anise / 2 cloves of garlic, cut in half / sea salt and freshly ground black pepper

Whisk the oil and vinegar together in a pan. Add all the herbs and spices and put on a low heat. Warm to about 50°C/100°F and remove from the heat. Cover with clingfilm and leave to infuse for about 12 hours. Pass through a muslin cloth. When needed, whisk well to emulsify.

WATER VINAIGRETTE INFUSED WITH TARRAGON

As everyone knows, water and oil don't mix, so the idea behind putting water into this vinaigrette is not just to lighten it up a bit but to get these lovely pearls of water on the plate after you've drizzled it around. This vinaigrette goes wonderfully with poached leeks. It has an indefinite shelf life — store it in an airtight container in the larder and shake well each time you use it. Makes 400ml.

300ml olive oil / 100ml white wine vinegar / sea salt and freshly ground black pepper / a large sprig of fresh tarragon

Whisk the oil and vinegar together, then add 50ml of water. Do not mix after this. Pour into a container, then season and add the tarragon. Leave to infuse overnight. When the vinaigrette is needed, spoon or ladle some of it, stirring very gently. The vinaigrette should marble into pearls on the plate.

RED PEPPER VINAIGRETTE

This vinaigrette is a lovely rosy colour and not as bright red as you'd imagine. It makes a great base for a pepper sauce and goes very well with fish and chicken. It has an indefinite shelf life – store it in an airtight container in the larder and shake well each time you use it. Makes 400ml.

2 red peppers / 300ml olive oil / 100ml white wine vinegar / sea salt and freshly ground black pepper

Core, deseed and slice the peppers. In a pan, sauté the peppers in 4 tablespoons of olive oil for 4–5 minutes. When soft, add the remaining oil and heat for a further 2 minutes. Leave to cool, then place in a container to steep. If possible leave for about 2 days, then strain the oil into a bowl. Whisk the vinegar and oil together and season.

ROCKET VINAIGRETTE

This vinaigrette is lovely and peppery and goes great with lobster. It has no shelf life, so you need to make it and use it straight away otherwise the rocket will turn the vinaigrette black. Makes 400ml.

300ml olive oil / 100ml white wine vinegar / 50g rocket / sea salt and freshly ground black pepper

Place all the ingredients into a blender and blitz for about 30 seconds until all the rocket is well blended. Season and pass through a muslin cloth. Mix well before using.

LEMON GRASS VINAIGRETTE

This vinaigrette is great with fish, most salads and anything you associate Thai flavouring with. To get the maximum flavour out of lemon grass you need to bruise the stalks with the back of a knife, or crush them. Warming the vinaigrette helps infuse it with the flavour of the lemon grass, as does leaving it to stand for 12 hours. This vinaigrette has an indefinite shelf life – store it in an airtight container in the larder and shake well each time you use it. Makes 400ml.

3 sticks of lemon grass / 300ml olive oil / 100ml white wine vinegar / sea salt and freshly ground black pepper

Finely bruise or crush the lemon grass. Whisk the oil and vinegar together in a pan and add the lemon grass. Put the pan on the stove and heat slowly to hand heat, then leave to infuse for about 12 hours. Pass the vinaigrette through a muslin cloth, and season. Stir well before using.

HONEY, SOY AND SESAME DRESSING

This dressing goes fantastically with chicken, and we've used it in the recipe for Warm oriental marinated chicken with king prawns and posh prawn toasts on page 22. The great thing about this dressing is that it can also be used as a marinade. It has an indefinite shelf life – store it in an airtight container in the larder and shake well each time you use it. Makes around 400ml.

100g honey / 10g English mustard / 100ml soy sauce / 20ml sherry vinegar / 50ml sesame oil / 100ml vegetable oil

Warm the honey and pour into a round-bottomed bowl. Whisk continuously and add all the remaining ingredients, finishing with the oils. The end result should be a nice smooth dressing somewhere between the consistency of a vinaigrette and a mayonnaise.

GRAIN MUSTARD AND CAPER DRESSING

This dressing is lovely over a new potato salad, or poured over fish such as skate. It has an indefinite shelf life – store it in an airtight container in the larder and shake well each time you use it. Makes 400ml.

300ml olive oil / 100ml white wine vinegar / 1 tablespoon grain mustard / 50g small capers in vinegar / sea salt and freshly ground black pepper

Whisk the oil and vinegar together. Add the mustard and mix well. Squeeze any excess vinegar from the capers, then mix into the vinaigrette and season.

HAZELNUT DRESSING

This dressing is perfect poured over quail or pigeon. It needs to be used on the same day it's made. Makes 500ml.

200ml red wine / 50ml sherry vinegar / 100ml hazelnut oil / 200ml olive oil / sea salt and freshly ground black pepper

Put the wine in a pan on a medium heat and boil to reduce down until you have a thick syrup. Using a spatula, scrape it into a rounded bowl. Whisk in the sherry vinegar and then add both the oils. Season to taste.

CHERRY TOMATO AND BALSAMIC DRESSING

This is a warm dressing which is more like a sauce. The trick here is to use very ripe tomatoes – almost overripe – to give it a lovely rich flavour. Also, be sure not to over-heat it as the butter may split and curdle. This dressing has no shelf life – you need to make it and use it straight away as it has cream and butter in it. Makes 250ml.

250g cherry vine tomatoes / 1 tablespoon balsamic vinegar / 2–3 small fresh basil leaves / 100ml double cream / 50g butter / sea salt and freshly ground black pepper / optional: 1 teaspoon caster sugar

Blitz the tomatoes, vinegar and basil in a blender. Pour through a sieve into a saucepan, rubbing with the back of a ladle. Cook uncovered until reduced by half. Mix in the cream then simmer for a minute or two before whisking in the butter a little at a time, until the mixture is nice and smooth. Pass through a sieve again and season to taste, adding a little sugar if necessary. Keep warm until needed.

LEMON AND BASIL INFUSED OLIVE OIL

This can be used pretty much in any salad dressing and is great drizzled over fish such as bream (see the Sea bream with roasted fennel, olives, clams, garlic and thyme recipe on page 112). Keeps for 3–4 days in the fridge. Makes 500ml.

zest of 2 washed lemons / 500ml good olive oil / 2 bunches of fresh basil

Peel the zest off the lemons in long thin strips. Place the olive oil and lemon zest in a pan and heat through gently. Add the basil and remove from the heat. Transfer to a clean container and cover with clingfilm. Leave to one side to infuse for 24 hours, then remove the basil and pour the oil and lemon zest into a screwtop jar until needed.

sauces, stocks & basics

'For me, sauces, stocks and basics are the most crucial elements to perfecting a dish'

When making sauces and stocks in the restaurant we ensure they are done to absolute perfection, because they are the kind of thing that can go wrong if you don't start off with the right love, care and attention. The thing with chicken stock is to skim it to prevent all the unwanted fat and scum boiling through the stock. And with stocks in general, if you don't caramelize the vegetables first, there will be no body or colouring to the stock. We don't use any form of extra colouring in our restaurant stocks; instead we depend heavily on roasting vegetables and browning onions.

When you make a stock you should season it at the beginning and then correct it at the end, as opposed to making the stock and then seasoning it as an after-thought. Think about seasoning in small doses along the way. It's also a good idea to use any trimmings in your stocks, for example, asparagus or leek in a vegetable stock. These leftover bits should never be discarded. Every scrap can be used.

Sauces are another great basic, and useful to know how to make. Hollandaise is a classic rich sauce that uses clarified butter. We've taken it a little bit further by finishing it with pink grapefruit or with mint. This way it's quite clean-tasting and less cloying on the palate. The main thing to watch out for when making hollandaise is not to let it split or become too grainy.

Every kitchen in Britain should be stocked with homemade mayonnaise. It is really important to be able to make a basic mayonnaise, and then you can season it accordingly, with tarragon, garlic, lemon or lime, or even a dash of Tabasco. A good tip is never to allow your mayonnaise to become too thin; it's better to start with a thicker consistency and thin it down.

CLASSIC MAYONNAISE

Once you've mastered this classic mayonnaise recipe you can take it in lots of different directions by adding other ingredients. I've listed the variations below, so have a go at making all of them. Keeps for 3 days in the fridge. Makes 300ml.

2 large free-range egg yolks / 1 teaspoon white wine vinegar / 1 teaspoon made English mustard / sea salt and freshly ground black pepper / 300ml groundnut oil

In a bowl whisk the egg yolks, vinegar, mustard and a pinch of salt. Slowly drizzle in the oil, whisking continuously until thick and emulsified. Check the seasoning and refrigerate before using.

VARIATIONS

- To make mousseline, fold 140ml of whipped cream through the mayonnaise to lighten it.
- For gribiche, add 1 chopped hard-boiled egg, 2 tablespoons of chopped capers and 2 tablespoons of chopped parsley.
- For watercress mayonnaise, add 3 tablespoons of fresh chopped watercress.
- And for anchovy mayonnaise, add 1 tablespoon of anchovy essence and 4 chopped anchovies.

GARLIC MAYONNAISE

This is great with all sorts of things: shellfish, king prawns, chicken, chips. Keeps for 3 days in the fridge. Makes 400ml.

100ml milk / 3 cloves of garlic, peeled / 2 free-range egg yolks / 1 teaspoon white wine vinegar / ½ teaspoon sea salt / freshly ground white or black pepper / 1 teaspoon English mustard / 300ml groundnut or salad oil

Put the milk into a pan with the garlic and heat gently. When the garlic is soft, sieve it into the egg yolks. Reserve the milk. Add the vinegar, salt, pepper and mustard and whisk together for a couple of minutes. Slowly whisk in the oil drop by drop, adding a little of the reserved milk to stop it splitting. Once all the oil has been added, season and pass through a fine sieve or tea strainer.

PINK GRAPEFRUIT HOLLANDAISE

This hollandaise goes great with fish, particularly trout and salmon. This must be made and used straight away. Makes 300ml.

6 coriander seeds, finely crushed / 3 egg yolks / 150ml light olive oil, warmed / juice of 1 lemon / sea salt / a pinch of cayenne pepper / 100ml fresh grapefruit juice / grated zest of 1 pink grapefruit

Put the crushed coriander seeds, egg yolks and 1 tablespoon of warm water into a heat-proof bowl and place the bowl over a saucepan of simmering water. Whisk the egg yolks until they are pale and creamy and form ribbons. Remove from the heat and whisk for a further 3 minutes, until the mixture has cooled slightly. Very slowly whisk in the oil in a steady drizzle. When finished, season with lemon juice, salt and a pinch of cayenne. Put the grapefruit juice and zest into a small pan and cook gently over a medium heat until the liquid has reduced to about 3 tablespoons. Whisk into the hollandaise.

MINT HOLLANDAISE

The thing to remember is never to allow a hollandaise to go cold because it will solidify and to bring it back to a warm creamy state is difficult. So leave it in a warm place, by the oven or next to the kettle. Don't even be scared to sit the bowl in your poaching liquor, to stop it from splitting. And if you think it's starting to split and won't hold until your guests arrive, take it to the tap and whisk it with cold water or drop an ice cube into it. This will bring it back together. Makes 300ml. Make and use straight away.

6 coriander seeds, finely crushed / 3 egg yolks / 2 teaspoons white wine vinegar / 200ml clarified butter (see page 244) / sea salt and freshly ground black pepper / a good pinch of cayenne pepper / a squeeze of fresh lemon juice / 2 teaspoons finely chopped fresh mint leaves

Put the crushed coriander seeds, egg yolks and 1 tablespoon of warm water into a heat-proof bowl and place the bowl over a saucepan of simmering water. Add the vinegar and whisk until the eggs form thick ribbons, then remove from the heat. Slowly drizzle in the clarified butter, whisking continuously until the butter disappears and the mixture becomes thick. Season with salt, pepper and cayenne. Add the lemon juice and mint and whisk in.

LAMB SAUCE

This sauce is obviously perfect for lamb, especially roast lamb. Keeps for 3 days in the fridge. Makes 3 litres.

2kg lamb bones / 100ml olive oil / 1 onion, chopped / 3 carrots, chopped / 2 celery sticks, chopped / ½ a head of garlic, chopped / a sprig of fresh thyme / 1 bay leaf / 1 tablespoon tomato purée / 250ml white wine / 4 litres brown chicken stock (see page 237)

Preheat the oven to 200°C/400°F/gas 6. Spread the lamb bones out in a roasting tray and roast for about 20 minutes, turning frequently.

Heat the olive oil in a large pan, add the vegetables, and cook until they are well coloured. Add the garlic, herbs and tomato purée, continue cooking for another 2–3 minutes, then add the wine. Cook for 7–8 minutes, until the wine has reduced by half and forms a syrup. Now add the lamb bones and the hot stock. Bring to the boil, then turn the heat down and simmer for 4 hours. Remove from the heat, pass through a sieve back into the pan and return to the heat until the sauce is thick enough to coat the back of a spoon.

SMOKED RED WINE SAUCE

This sauce is good with pan-fried fish such as salmon, brill or bream. It also goes nicely with roast lobster. Keeps for 3 days in the fridge. Makes 285ml.

2 tablespoons olive oil / 8 shallots, sliced / a sprig of fresh thyme / 1 bay leaf / 12 peppercorns / 50g smoked bacon, diced / 1 teaspoon smoked paprika / 1 tablespoon sherry vinegar / 75ml red wine / 565ml fish stock

Put the olive oil into a pan, add the shallots, herbs, peppercorns, bacon and paprika, and sauté until caramelized. Pour in the vinegar, stir well, then add the red wine. Continue cooking until it reduces to a syrup, then add the fish stock and cook until reduced by half. Pass the liquid twice through a muslin cloth to remove all the solids and leave you with a lovely smooth sauce.

SAUCE DIABLE

'Diable' means devil in French, so unsurprisingly this is quite a spicy, hot sauce. It goes really well with beef or pork. Keeps for 3 days in the fridge. Makes 140ml.

285ml white wine / 2 tablespoons white wine vinegar / 20g chopped shallots / 200ml brown chicken stock (see page 237) / cayenne pepper

Put the wine, vinegar and shallots into a large pan and cook over a medium heat until you are left with a third of the liquid you started with. Add the stock and bring to the boil, then continue cooking until you have a sauce consistency. Season with enough cayenne to make it nice and spicy!

WHITE WINE CHICKEN STOCK WITH TURNIPS

This stock is great for almost anything: fish, beef or pork. Use it as a base for stews or soups, or for poaching chicken. The turnips will add a great flavour to the stock but won't be overbearing. Keeps for 3 days in the fridge or 1 month in the freezer. Makes 5 litres. For a brown chicken stock recipe, see page 237.

3kg chicken carcasses, chopped / 5 litres cold water / 1 tablespoon salt / 300ml white wine / 3 onions, roughly chopped / 2 leeks, roughly chopped / 3 large carrots, roughly chopped / 4 celery sticks, roughly chopped / 1 small head of garlic, cloves halved but not peeled / 1 sprig of fresh thyme / 8 large turnips, quartered

Place the chicken carcasses and water in a large pan. Bring to the boil, skimming well every so often to remove the white residue from the surface. Add all the other ingredients except the turnips. Reduce the heat, simmer for 3 hours, then add the turnips. Simmer for a further hour, then leave to cool before passing through a sieve.

PARSNIP STOCK FLAVOURED WITH THYME

This is best used as a base stock for a parsnip risotto. Keeps for 3 days in the fridge or 5 days in the freezer. Makes 2 litres.

10 large parsnips / olive oil / 10 large shallots, sliced / a bunch of fresh thyme / 2 cloves of garlic / 10 white peppercorns / a pinch of curry powder / 2 litres good chicken stock

Wash and chop the parsnips but don't peel them. Heat a little olive oil in a large pan and cook the shallots, thyme, garlic, peppercorns and curry powder until softened. Add the parsnips and the stock and bring to the boil. Simmer for 30–40 minutes, then pass through a sieve.

FISH STOCK INFUSED WITH VANILLA

It's best to use bones from white fish for this — turbot bones tend to make the best stock. This recipe is a good one for using up leftover vanilla pods when you may have used the seeds for something else. Never throw away the pods! This stock goes wonderfully with sea bass. For a straightforward fish stock, leave out the vanilla. Keeps for 3 days in the fridge or 1 month in the freezer. Makes 3 litres.

olive oil / 1 onion, roughly chopped / 1 large leek, roughly chopped / 1 celery stick, roughly chopped / 1 fennel bulb, roughly chopped / 2 cloves of garlic, chopped / 2kg fish bones, chopped / 300ml white wine / 3 litres cold water / 1 sprig of fresh thyme / 1 bay leaf / 10 white peppercorns / 1 lemon, sliced / 2 vanilla pods

Heat a little olive oil in a large pan, add all the vegetables and the garlic, and cook gently for about 10 minutes. Add the fish bones and the wine, and cook until reduced by two-thirds. Add the water, thyme, bay leaf and peppercorns and bring to the boil, skimming off any residue, then add the lemon slices and the vanilla pods. Reduce the heat and simmer gently for 20 minutes. Leave to stand for 5 minutes, then strain.

COURT-BOUILLON

This is the ideal stock to use for poaching fish and shellfish, and you can actually use it three times. After you've used it the first time, pass it through a sieve and store it in the fridge. You can then use it twice more as a poaching liquor before you'll need to throw it away. Keeps for 3 days in the fridge or 1 month in the freezer. Makes 3 litres.

2 large leeks / 3 large carrots / 3 onions / 2 sticks of celery / 2 fennel bulbs / 4 cloves of garlic / a sprig of fresh thyme / a sprig of fresh parsley / a sprig of fresh basil / a sprig of fresh tarragon / 2 lemons, sliced / 4 star anise / 300ml white wine / 3 litres cold water / 1 tablespoon sea salt

Peel all the vegetables and the garlic and chop into very small pieces. Place in a large pan and add the rest of the ingredients. Bring to the boil, then reduce the heat and simmer for 30 minutes. Leave to stand for a couple of hours, or overnight if possible, before using.

LEMON CONFIT

Lemon confit has a multitude of uses. Lay some slices on top of a roast chicken about 5 minutes before it's cooked. Or use it to finish pan-fried fish. Lemon confit keeps for 1 month and should be kept in the fridge at all times. Makes 20 slices.

2 large unwaxed lemons, washed / 100g caster sugar / a stalk of lemon grass, halved

Using a sharp carving knife or a Japanese slicer, cut the lemons into thin, even slices. Remove any pips, being careful to keep the membrane intact. Put the sugar in a pan over a medium heat, add 300ml of water and stir till dissolved. Add the lemon grass, bring to the boil, then reduce the heat and simmer for 2–3 minutes. Add the lemon slices and poach gently for 8–10 minutes, then remove from the heat and leave to cool. Store in a screw-top jar in their liquid until needed.

CLASSIC PESTO

This dressing can be used for lots of things. It's great with fish, can be mixed through pasta, and is even used to finish soups such as minestrone (see page 90). Keeps for 5 days in the fridge. Makes 250ml.

50g pine nuts / 70g fresh basil leaves / 3 cloves of garlic, peeled / 50g Parmesan cheese / 125ml olive oil / sea salt and freshly ground black pepper

Toast the pine nuts in a small pan, then remove from the pan and leave to cool. Place them in a blender with the basil, garlic and Parmesan and give them a quick blitz. Scrape down the sides and then, with the machine running, slowly add the oil, scraping down the sides occasionally. When all the oil has been added, check the seasoning – add a little salt and some black pepper if needed.

TARAMASALATA

This recipe is nothing like the homogenized stuff you buy in shops, which is made with salmon roe and is actually dyed pink. I don't know why on earth they insist on doing this – it looks so unappetizing! I use cod roe in my taramasalata, and it's so much more creamy and has a lovely smoky flavour to it. We serve it at Claridge's with crevettes, as a canapé. Delicious. Keeps for 5 days in the fridge. Makes approximately 850ml.

135g smoked cod roe / 1½ lemons, juiced / 2½ slices of white bread / 1 clove of garlic, crushed / 75ml milk / 550ml vegetable oil

Remove and discard any hard pieces of skin from the cod roe, then purée it in a food processor with the lemon juice, bread, garlic and milk. With the mix still processing, slowly add the oil. If the mixture seems a little too oily at the end, just add a little more milk.

ESSENTIAL TECHNIQUES

HOW TO POACH AN EGG

The most important thing here is to use amazingly fresh eggs. If the eggs aren't fresh to start with, you'll never get anywhere. You can tell that an egg is fresh if when you crack it the majority of the white clings to the yolk. If the egg white is watery and comes away from the yolk, then you know it's not fresh. It's the same when you poach it – with a fresh egg all the egg white sticks to the yolk and you get a lovely round shape, but if it's watery it will strand out and rise to the top in a horrible foam.

Trick number one when poaching an egg is to have a nice deep pan of boiling water, and it needs to be well seasoned with white wine vinegar. You can use malt vinegar if you don't have white wine vinegar, but this means the poached egg will be slightly coloured. Vinegar helps to strengthen the albumen (protein) in the egg white, which sets it and gives it that lovely shape.

Trick number two is to break each egg into a separate cup first, so you know if the yolk is broken. This also makes it easier to tip it into the water.

Using a slotted spoon, stir the boiling water in the pan around to make a well in the centre, then drop the egg into it. It will fall through the well and spin around. Cook the egg for 3–4 minutes. You should only poach a maximum of 4 eggs at a time – just make sure the well is spinning quite fast and drop each egg in separately.

When making the Ultimate Caesar salad (see page 18) you can get the poached eggs ready before you start. For this recipe the eggs are perfectly done when the yolks are very springy to touch and you can tell they're undercooked right in the centre. Remove them from the pan and plunge them into iced water to stop the cooking process. When they've cooled slightly, take them out of the water and trim any stray bits of egg white so you get a really smooth shape. Lay them on some kitchen paper or a clean cloth, cover them with clingfilm, and put them in the fridge until you need them. When you are ready to use them, plunge them back into boiling water to reheat for approximately 2 minutes.

HOW TO MAKE A BROWN CHICKEN STOCK

White chicken stock looks quite anaemic, so in order to give it more depth of colour the first thing to do is brown the chicken carcass. This also gives the stock a lot more flavour.

Chicken stock is great to use in recipes that usually use veal stock, and is far easier to make and less cloying on the palate. It's great for sauces, stews and soups such as French onion. It will keep for 1 week in the fridge in a sealed container. Makes 1 litre.

1 chicken carcass / 1 carrot / 1 onion / 2 sticks of celery / 1 leek / vegetable oil / a sprig of thyme / 1 bay leaf / 3 cloves of garlic, peeled / 2 tablespoons tomato purée / 2 tablespoons white flour

Preheat the oven to 200°C/400°F/gas mark 6. Place the chicken carcass in a roasting tray and put it into the oven for 15–20 minutes.

Chop the carrot, onion, celery and leek into large chunks. Heat some oil in a pan and add the chopped vegetables, along with the thyme, bay leaf and garlic. Sauté for a few minutes until golden brown, stirring frequently. Add the tomato purée and cook for another 4–5 minutes until the mixture is a rich brown colour.

Five minutes before taking the chicken carcass out of the oven, lightly dust it with flour. The flour not only acts as a thickening agent to the stock but also stops it becoming greasy, as it soaks up all the excess fat. This way the stock becomes really beautiful and transparent. Return the carcass to the oven for the final 5 minutes, then pick the bones out of the tray and add them to the pan of vegetables. Top up the pan with just enough cold water to cover the bones. It's very important to use cold water so that any fat or grease left on the vegetables or bones will solidify and rise to the surface, where you can skim it off. If you use boiling water it will disperse the fat throughout the stock. Bring the stock to the boil, turn the heat down, skim the scum off the top and let it simmer for an hour. Pass through a sieve.

HOW TO DRY SALAD LEAVES

The reason it's so important to dry lettuce leaves is because this is the best way to dress them – when they're at least 90 per cent dry. You don't need to worry about washing salad leaves such as iceberg, which are grown in greenhouses, and it's also not necessary to wash baby spinach; however, you do need to wash normal spinach quite thoroughly, and you should always taste a little to ensure you've managed to wash away all the dirt. The easiest way to tell if salad leaves are clean is to drain them in a colander after you've washed them and check the colour of the water.

The best way to dry salad leaves is to wash them first, then dip them into iced water for 10 seconds to help them stay crisp. Don't leave them in the iced water, as this will make them soggy. Then put the salad into a clean tea towel, gather up the corners and spin it around. (Please don't use a salad spinner or the leaves will bruise.) Once you've dried them, put a damp cloth over them to keep them fresh until you need them.

HOW TO FILLET, PINBONE AND SKIN FISH

It's best to give the job of filleting a fish to the fishmonger, but with some fish, such as salmon, you may also need to remove fine hair bones. This is known as pinboning. Remember, some fish is a lot easier to pinbone when cooked – if you struggle to do it while it's raw you'll end up ripping the fish. Lay your fish fillet flat on a board. Using a vegetable peeler, slide each individual hair bone between its blades and flick upwards, loosening it and pulling it away from the flesh. Continue this method until you have removed all the hair bones from the fillet. There are some fish, such as sardines, that you don't need to pinbone at all – the bones are so soft you can actually eat them.

When skinning a fish, make sure you use a sharp, flexible knife. Lay your fish on a board skin side down. With one hand pinch the tail between your fingers; with the other use your knife to make an incision in the skin, crossways and just above the tail. Slide the knife under the skin and make long slicing motions towards the head of the fish at a slight downward angle, lifting the skin away from the flesh as you go along. You should always skin a fish from tail to head.

HOW TO PAN-FRY FISH IN BROWN BUTTER

Frying fish in butter gives it a lovely nutty flavour. Start by lightly dusting your fish with flour. Heat 2 tablespoons of olive oil in a pan until very hot and brown the presentation side of the fish first for 2–3 minutes, depending upon its size. Turn the fish over, add 5 knobs of butter to the pan, and fry for a further 2–3 minutes. By the time the fish is cooked the butter should be foaming and a lovely brown colour. By adding the butter at this later stage it doesn't have a chance to burn and turn black and gritty.

HOW TO KILL AND REMOVE THE CLAWS AND TAIL FROM A LOBSTER

Kill the lobster humanely by putting a knife in the back of its head, between its eyes. Then cut downwards in a quick smooth motion (i.e. cutting the head in half, lengthways). After that it's just a matter of ripping the claws off and wiggling off the tail until it comes away from the head.

HOW TO MAKE DELICIOUS MASHED POTATO

The best potatoes to use are waxy ones, ideally Desirée. Peel and cut up 1kg of potatoes into even-sized chunks and poach them gently in salted water. Put plenty of salt in the water (as long as you don't make it ridiculously salty, like sea water) as it gives a much better flavour to the potatoes. Don't boil them, but poach them gently until they're cooked, probably for about 45 minutes. Then drain them and put them back in the pan, shaking them around over the heat for 3–4 minutes to dry them out. While they're still hot, push them through a sieve. Mix 140ml milk with 140ml cream in a pan and bring to the boil. Add 200g softened butter to the potato purée and then slowly incorporate the milk, a ladleful at a time. Add as much or as little milk as you need to get the texture you require: firmer if you're serving with meat and wetter if you're serving with fish. Check the seasoning again and add salt if it needs it. To get a really fine texture, pass the purée through a clean sieve again to remove any lumpy bits.

HOW TO MAKE CRISPY CHIPS

The best potatoes to use are Desirée. Cut them to the thickness you require. Put enough vegetable oil in a deep pan to cover the chips and heat to 130°C/250°F. Add the chips and cook until they're almost tender but haven't taken on any colour. Remove from the oil, drain, and if you don't need them right away put them in the fridge until you do. Just before serving, raise the temperature of the oil to 180°C/350°F and cook the chips until golden brown. Do a handful at a time so as not to reduce the temperature of the oil. Remove the chips from the oil and drain off the excess fat on kitchen paper before serving.

HOW TO MAKE A SUGAR OR STOCK SYRUP

In a heavy-bottomed pan, combine 3 parts sugar with 1 part water. Bring to the boil, then turn the heat down and simmer for 10 minutes until all the sugar has dissolved and the mixture has become syrupy in consistency.

GLOSSARY

Al dente In Italian means 'to the tooth'. Pasta when it's just cooked.

Bain-marie A cooking method whereby a dish is put inside a baking tray half to three-quarters full of water, then put into the oven so that the food cooks gently and evenly.

Baste A method usually used when roasting. The food is coated continuously with the oil or fat it's being cooked in.

Batons Vegetables cut into large matchstick shapes.

Beurre noisette A stage of butter after being heated for a while. The solids and fat separate and the butter takes on a nut-brown colour. Usually used with fish.

Blanch This has two meanings: to pre-cook vegetables or pasta briefly in water; or to pre-cook potato chips in fat at a lower temperature in order to make them nice and crispy when the cooking is finished later in hot fat.

Bouquet garni A bundle of herbs (usually thyme, bay leaf, garlic, clove, parsley) tied with string and used in stocks, sauces and soups to flavour.

Braise A cooking method usually used for tougher cuts of meat to make them tender. The food is cooked slowly in liquid, generally in an oven.

Caramelize Either cooking sugar in a heavy bottomed pan until it turns to a caramel, or roasting vegetables, such as onions, until they take on a nice golden colour.

Clarified butter A clear yellow fat which is the result of warming butter in a heavy-bottomed pan very slowly over a low heat until it separates. Pass through a muslin cloth to separate the solid and whey skin from the yellow fat, which you can then heat to very high temperatures without burning.

Confit A slow process of cooking something submerged in liquid, or to cook duck or goose in its own fat.

Court-bouillon A vegetable stock flavoured with spices such as coriander, star anise and lemon, used as a poaching liquor to cook mainly fish such as lobster, langoustine or salmon.

Daube A cooking method used to tenderize tougher meats.

Deglaze To add wine, vinegar or stock to a pan in which meat or vegetables have been cooked, in order to dilute the remaining juices to make a sauce or gravy.

Emulsion A mixture of butter and water used as a reheating liquor for vegetables. Mainly used for poaching fish.

Emulsify To bring ingredients together to make a stable liquid.

Fondant A cooking technique mainly used with hard vegetables, whereby you cook the vegetables in foaming butter or stock in the oven until soft.

Glaze Coating something with sugar or butter that sets or hardens to give a glossy surface.

Goujons Posh word for fish fingers. Strips of fish coated in egg and breadcrumbs and deep-fried.

Gratinate To cook something, usually containing cream, cheese or egg yolk, under a hot grill until bubbling and golden.

Infuse To impart the flavour of something into warm liquid.

Japanese slicer A piece of kitchen equipment used to slice vegetables diagonally.

Julienne Very thin vegetable strips, usually carrot or leek.

Lardons Uniform strips of pancetta or streaky bacon.

Mandolin A piece of kitchen equipment used for slicing.

Pinbone To remove the very fine bones from fish such as salmon.

Poach To cook in hot liquid, usually water or stock.

Purée To blend until smooth.

Quenelle A shape made with mousse or cream using two spoons.

Ragú A tomato-based sauce.

Reduce To boil liquid down, usually by two-thirds, until syrupy.

Refresh To plunge into iced water.

Roast To cook food in an oven, or to give colour to food by cooking in a pan on the stove.

Sabayon Egg yolks and sugar beaten with an electric mixer until light and frothy.

Salamander Another name for a grill.

Sauté To fry in oil or butter.

Score To cut the skin of a fish with a sharp knife in order to aid the cooking process.

Season To flavour with salt or pepper.

Simmer To cook at just under boiling point so that the surface is bubbling gently.

Skim To remove the fat or scum that forms on a stock with a ladle.

Sugar syrup A mixture of sugar and water, usually three parts sugar to one part water, heated in a pan until the sugar has dissolved. Also known as stock syrup.

Velouté French word for a soup or sauce, generally cream-based.

Zest The grated skin of citrus fruits.

ACKNOWLEDGEMENTS

My thanks to the team at Penguin — John Hamilton, Art Director, who with the knowledge he acquired during the production of this book can now make a career change to bloody good Head Chef; the gorgeous ladies Lindsey Jordan, Editorial Director, and her editorial assistant Chantal Gibbs, who while editing my recipes in the kitchens proved a great distraction to my kitchen brigade; and Lis Parsons and Mark Read for managing to capture the true unmanufactured, unstyled me in their photographs. And a huge thank you to Annie Lee, the copy editor, Sarah Day, Editorial Manager, Chris Callard, the designer and Tiina Wastie in Production.

In appreciation for all the support from Optomen Television — the dynamic Pat Llewellyn, Executive Producer and now experienced rolled-up-sleeve pot-and-pan washer; hands-on Series Producer Christine Hall for keeping me and my time-keeping in line — also for instructing me in the art of texting during long train journeys; cameraman Danny and sound engineer Simon, the best professional silent shadows, for picking up my every move in the cramped kitchen areas; and Martha and Sasha for their phenomenal energy, which complemented the Optomen team.

To my PA Lynne Brenner, whose diary management has now pushed her to the limits of trying to source a Gordon Ramsay 'double'. I could propose my son, Jack, aged four, but it will be at least another ten years (Heaven forbid!) before another Ramsay is let loose in the kitchen! Last but not least to the creativity of Mark Sargeant (aka Sarge). The more pressure he takes on the better he becomes.

Finally, to my wife, Tana, for allowing me to sneak in photoshoots at weekends and work seven days a week so that this book would be completed in time for publication. And to the Godfather — Chris Hutcheson, Gordon Ramsay Holdings.

INDEX

a

à la Grecque 217

apples
    calvados rice pudding with
        caramelized 200
    and cardamom tarte Tatin
        with cardamom ice cream 195
    smoked ham hock, celeriac,
        apple and endive salad 26

artichokes
    Jerusalem artichoke risotto with
        scallops 128

asparagus
    baked asparagus and Parmesan
        loaf 78
    poached sea trout with asparagus
        and mint hollandaise 115

aubergines
    salad of tomatoes with aubergine
        caviar and coriander cress 76

b

bacon
    butter bean, bacon and parsley
        soup 102

baked asparagus and Parmesan
    loaf 78

baked pumpkin 66

banana
    soufflés 191–2
    sticky toffee pudding 192

bang bang chicken 174

basil
    grilled plum tomatoes with
        baby mozzarella, basil and
        olive oil 44
    lemon and basil infused
        olive oil 221

beans
    butter bean, bacon and
        parsley soup 102

gorgonzola risotto with peas
    and broad 61

beef
    burger and chips 158
    cottage pie 162
    lasagne 165
    sirloin of beef with roasted Charlotte
        potatoes and red wine shallots 156

beetroot
    roast skate with beetroot and
        Parmesan 124

black forest gateau 202

bouillabaisse 138

braised Belgian endive 75

braised lentils with Swiss chard, turnips
    and parsley ravioli 83

braised oxtail in beef tomatoes 155

braised shank of lamb with parsnip
    purée 148

bread
    grilled flat mushrooms and pancetta
        on toasted brioche with Welsh
        rarebit 42
    grilled plum tomatoes with baby
        mozzarella, basil and olive oil 44
    grilled sardines and chunky provençal
        tomato sauce on toasted poilane 40
    lobster roll 46
    mackerel on toast with a warm
        potato salad 50
    roasted suckling pig with coleslaw and
        rocket on granary 47
    smoked salmon and cream cheese
        croque monsieur 53

bread and butter pudding, whisky 208

bream with roasted fennel, olives,
    clams, garlic and thyme 112

broad beans
    gorgonzola risotto with peas
        and broad 61

burger and chips 158

butter bean, bacon and parsley soup 102

c

Caesar salad 18

cake
  black forest gateau 202
  pear financier 207
  calvados rice pudding with caramelized
      apples 200

capers
  grain mustard and caper dressing 219

caramelized pineapple with sherbet 187

cardamom
  apple and cardamom tarte Tatin with
      cardamom ice cream 195

carrots
  lamb stew with parsley dumplings
      and young 166

celeriac
  smoked ham hock, celeriac, apple
      and endive salad 26

cèpes
  pheasant baked with 168

cheese
  baked asparagus and Parmesan
      loaf 78
  gorgonzola risotto with peas
      and broad beans 61
  grilled plum tomatoes with baby
      mozzarella, basil and olive oil 44
  pumpkin and Parmesan soup 98
  roast skate with beetroot
      and Parmesan 124
  twice baked cheese soufflés
      69

cherry tomato and balsamic dressing 221

chicken
  bang bang 174
  poached chicken legs with
      herb dumplings and turnips 152
  warm oriental marinated chicken
      with king prawns and posh
      prawn toasts 22

chicken stock
  brown 237

white wine chicken stock with
      turnips 232

chips 241

chocolate
  mousse with lavender ice cream 196
  and toffee fondant 193

chorizo
  cod with 132

clams
  sea bream with roasted fennel, olives,
      clams, garlic and thyme 112

cod with chorizo 132

coleslaw
  roasted suckling pig with coleslaw
      and rocket on granary 47

coriander
  fillet of trout roasted with lemon and
      coriander, with spicy couscous 17
  coriander cress
  salad of tomatoes with aubergine
      caviar and 76

cottage pie 162

court-bouillon 233

couscous
  fillet of trout roasted with lemon
      and coriander, with spicy 17

crab and ginger salad with baby gem,
      lemon confit and fennel shavings 30

cream cheese
  smoked salmon and cream cheese
      croque monsieur 53

crème brûlée
  mint crème brûlée with
      strawberries 184

crispy duck salad 28

d

daube of squid 134

diable sauce 232

Dover sole with mashed potato
    and French peas 116

dressings
  cherry tomato and balsamic 221
  grain mustard and caper 219

hazelnut 219
honey, soy and sesame 219
mustard and honey 26
duck
crispy duck salad 28
marinated duck breasts 177
dumplings
herb 152
parsley 166

e

eggs
poached 236
poached salmon niçoise with
boiled quail's 21
smoked haddock soup with quail's 99
endive
braised Belgian 75
smoked ham hock, celeriac,
apple and endive salad 26

f

fennel
crab and ginger salad with baby gem,
lemon confit and fennel shavings 30
sea bream with roasted fennel, olives,
clams, garlic and thyme 112
fish
bouillabaisse 138
cream 121
filleting, pinboning and skinning 240
pan-frying in brown butter 240
pie 127
stock infused with vanilla 233
(see also individual names)
French onion soup 96

g

garlic mayonnaise 228
gazpacho, roasted pepper 105
ginger
crab and ginger salad with baby gem,
lemon confit and fennel shavings 30
gorgonzola risotto with peas
and broad beans 61

grain mustard and caper dressing 219
grapefruit see pink grapefruit
grapes
halibut on a bed of spinach with Muscat
grapes and fish cream 121
gratin
tomato, onion and potato 74
grilled flat mushrooms and pancetta on
toasted brioche with Welsh rarebit 42
grilled lobster and chips 122
grilled plum tomatoes with baby
mozzarella, basil and olive oil 44
grilled sardines and chunky
provençal tomato sauce on toasted
poilane bread 40
grilled vegetable salad marinated in
lemon and basil oil 32

h

haddock, smoked see smoked haddock
halibut on a bed of spinach with Muscat
grapes and fish cream 121
ham
smoked ham hock, celeriac, apple
and endive salad 26
hazelnut dressing 219
herb dumplings 152
hollandaise
mint 229
pink grapefruit 229
honey
mustard and honey dressing 26
and soy and sesame dressing 219

i

ice cream
cardamom 195
lavender 196

j

Jerusalem artichoke risotto
with scallops 128

l

lamb
  braised shank of lamb with
    parsnip purée 148
  sauce 230
  stew with parsley dumplings
    and young carrots 166
lasagne 165
lavender ice cream 196
leeks
  vinaigrette of leeks with pink grapefruit
    hollandaise 62
lemon
  and basil infused olive oil 221
  confit 235
  crab and ginger salad with baby gem,
    lemon confit and fennel shavings 30
  fillet of trout roasted with lemon and
    coriander, with spicy couscous 17
lemon grass vinaigrette 218
lentils
  braised lentils with Swiss chard,
    turnips and parsley ravioli 83
lobster
  grilled lobster and chips 122
  killing and removing claws
    and tail from 240
  roll 46

m

mackerel on toast with a warm
  potato salad 50
marinated duck breasts 177
marrow
  turnip, marrow and potato soup 95
mashed potato 241
mayonnaise
  classic 228
  garlic 228
minestrone 90
mint
  crème brûlée with
    strawberries 184
  hollandaise 229

  poached sea trout with
    asparagus and mint hollandaise 115
mousse
  chocolate mousse with lavender ice
    cream 196
mozzarella
  grilled plum tomatoes with baby
    mozzarella, basil and olive oil 44
mushrooms
  grilled flat mushrooms and pancetta
    on toasted brioche with Welsh
    rarebit 42
  pheasant baked with cèpes 168
mustard
  grain mustard and caper dressing 219
  and honey dressing 26

o

olive oil
  lemon and basil infused 221
olives
  sea bream with roasted fennel, olives,
    clams, garlic and thyme 112
onion(s)
  French onion soup 96
  relish 158
  tomato, onion and potato
    gratin 74
oxtail
  braised oxtail in beef tomatoes 155

p

pancetta
  grilled flat mushrooms and pancetta
    on toasted brioche with Welsh
    rarebit 42
Parmesan
  baked asparagus and Parmesan
    loaf 78
  pumpkin and Parmesan soup 98
  roast skate with beetroot
    and 124
parsley
  butter bean, bacon and
    parsley soup 102
  dumplings 166

parsnip
 braised shank of lamb with
  parsnip purée 148
 stock flavoured with thyme 232
pasta
 braised lentils with Swiss chard,
  turnips and parsley ravioli 83
 lasagne 165
 penne with cherry tomato sauce 72
pear financier 207
peas
 Dover sole with mashed
  potato and French 116
 gorgonzola risotto with peas
  and broad beans 61
penne with cherry tomato sauce 72
peppers
 braised in red wine 80
 red pepper vinaigrette 218
 roasted pepper gazpacho 105
pesto 235
pheasant baked with cèpes 168
pie, venison 171
pineapple
 caramelized pineapple with sherbet 187
pink grapefruit hollandaise 229
 vinaigrette of leeks with 62
pizza, puff pastry 70
poached chicken legs with herb
 dumplings and turnips 152
poached eggs 236
poached salmon niçoise with boiled
 quail's eggs 21
poached sea trout with asparagus
 and mint hollandaise 115
pork
 roasted suckling pig with coleslaw
  and rocket on granary 47
 stuffed loin of roast suckling pig with
  crispy crackling 146
potatoes
 chips 241
 Dover sole with mashed potato
  and French peas 116
 grilled lobster and chips 122

mackerel on toast with a warm
 potato salad 50
mashed 241
sirloin of beef with roasted Charlotte
 potatoes and red wine shallots 156
tomato, onion and potato
 gratin 74
turnip, marrow and potato
 soup 95
prawns
 warm oriental marinated chicken
  with king prawns and posh prawn
  toasts 22
puddings
 apple and cardamom tarte Tatin
  with cardamom ice cream 195
 banana soufflés 191–2
 banana sticky toffee 192
 black forest gateau 202
 calvados rice pudding with
  caramelized apples 200
 caramelized pineapple with
  sherbet 187
 chocolate mousse with
  lavender ice cream 196
 chocolate and toffee fondant
  193
 mint crème brûlée with
  strawberries 184
 pear financier 207
 whisky bread and butter 208
puff pastry pizza 70
pumpkin
 baked 66
 and Parmesan soup 98

q
quail's eggs
 poached salmon niçoise with
  boiled 21
 smoked haddock soup with 99

r
ravioli
 braised lentils with Swiss chard,
  turnips and parsley 83

red pepper vinaigrette 218

red wine

  peppers braised in 80

  sirloin of beef with roasted Charlotte
    potatoes and red wine shallots 156

  smoked red wine sauce 230

rice

  gorgonzola risotto with peas
    and broad beans 61

  Jerusalem artichoke risotto with scallops
    128

rice pudding

  calvados rice pudding with caramelized
    apples 200

risotto

  gorgonzola risotto with peas
    and broad beans 61

  Jerusalem artichoke risotto
    with scallops 128

roast skate with beetroot and
  Parmesan 124

roasted pepper gazpacho 105

roasted suckling pig with coleslaw and
  rocket on granary 47

rocket

  roasted suckling pig with coleslaw and
    rocket on granary 47

  vinaigrette 218

S

salad leaves, drying 237, 240

salads

  Caesar 18

  crab and ginger salad with baby gem,
    lemon confit and fennel shavings 30

  crispy duck 28

  fillet of trout roasted with lemon and
    coriander, with spicy couscous 17

  grilled vegetable salad marinated in
    lemon and basil oil 32

  poached salmon niçoise with boiled
    quail's eggs 21

  smoked ham hock, celeriac, apple
    and endive 26

  of tomatoes with aubergine
    caviar and coriander cress 76

  warm oriental marinated chicken
    with king prawns and posh prawn
    toasts 22

salmon

  poached salmon niçoise with boiled
    quail's eggs 21

sardines

  grilled sardines and chunky provençal
    tomato sauce on toasted poilane
    bread 40

sauces

  diable 232

  lamb 230

  mint hollandaise 229

  pink grapefruit hollandaise
    229

  smoked red wine 230

  scallops

  Jerusalem artichoke risotto with 128

sea trout

  poached sea trout with asparagus and
    mint hollandaise 115

sirloin of beef with roasted Charlotte
  potatoes and red wine shallots 156

skate

  roast skate with beetroot and Parmesan
    124

smoked haddock soup with quail's eggs
  99

smoked ham hock, celeriac, apple and
  endive salad 26

smoked red wine sauce 230

smoked salmon and cream cheese
  croque monsieur 53

soufflés

  banana 191–2

  twice baked cheese 69

soups

  bouillabaisse 138

  butter bean, bacon and parsley 102

  French onion 96

  minestrone 90

  pumpkin and Parmesan 98

roasted pepper gazpacho 105

smoked haddock soup with
   quail's eggs 99

turnip, marrow and potato 95

spinach
   halibut on a bed of spinach with Muscat
      grapes and fish cream 121

squid, daube of 134

stock
   brown chicken 237
   court-bouillon 233
   fish stock infused with vanilla 233
   parsnip stock flavoured with thyme 232
   white wine chicken stock
      with turnips 232

strawberries
   mint crème brûlée with 184

stuffed loin of roast suckling pig
   with crispy crackling 146

suckling pig
   roasted suckling pig with
      coleslaw and rocket on granary 47
   stuffed loin of roast suckling pig
      with crispy crackling 146

sugar syrup 241

Swiss chard
   braised lentils with Swiss chard,
      turnips and parsley ravioli 83

t

taramasalata 235

tarragon
   water vinaigrette infused with 217

tarte Tatin
   apple and cardamom tarte Tatin with
      cardamom ice cream 195

toffee pudding, banana sticky 192

tomato(es)
   braised oxtail in beef 155
   cherry tomato and balsamic
      dressing 221
   grilled plum tomatoes with baby
      mozzarella, basil and olive oil 44
   grilled sardines and chunky provençal
      tomato sauce on toasted poilane
      bread 40

and onion and potato gratin 74

penne with cherry tomato sauce 72

salad of tomatoes with aubergine caviar
   and coriander cress 76

trout
   fillet of trout roasted with lemon and
      coriander, with spicy couscous 17
   poached sea trout with
      asparagus and mint hollandaise 115

turnip(s)
   braised lentils with Swiss chard,
      turnips and parsley ravioli 83
   and marrow and potato soup 95
   poached chicken legs with herb
      dumplings and 152
   white wine chicken stock with 232

twice baked cheese soufflés 69

v

vegetables
   grilled vegetable salad marinated in
      lemon and basil oil 32

venison pie 171

vinaigrette
   à la Grecque 217
   classic 217
   lemon grass 218
   red pepper 218
   rocket 218
   water vinaigrette infused
      with tarragon 217
   vinaigrette of leeks with pink grapefruit
      hollandaise 62

w

warm oriental marinated chicken
   with king prawns and posh
   prawn toasts 22

water vinaigrette infused
   with tarragon 217

whisky bread and butter pudding 208

white wine chicken stock
   with turnips 232